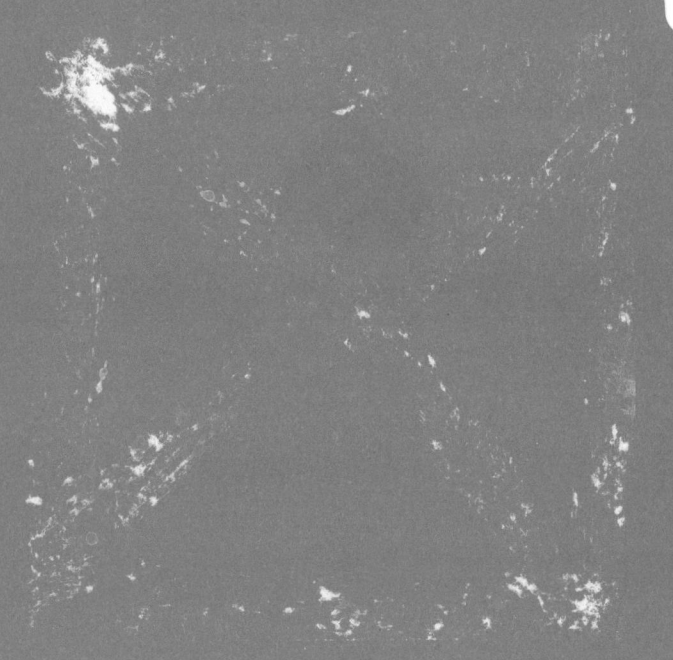

A Big Country

KATHIE ATKINSON

A Big Country

Stories of Australia
& its people from the ABC-TV series

Jim Downes

Unless otherwise indicated, photographs were obtained from the archives of the Australian Broadcasting Corporation. The assistance of the archivist, Pat Kelly, is gratefully acknowledged.

ANGUS & ROBERTSON PUBLISHERS

*Unit 4, Eden Park, 31 Waterloo Road,
North Ryde, NSW, Australia 2113;
94 Newton Road, Auckland 1,
New Zealand; and
16 Golden Square, London W1R, 4BN,
United Kingdom*

*This book is copyright.
Apart from any fair dealing for the
purposes of private study, research,
criticism or review, as permitted
under the Copyright Act, no part may
be reproduced by any process without
written permission. Inquiries should
be addressed to the publishers.*

*First published in Australia
by Angus & Robertson Publishers
and ABC Enterprises (for the Australian
Broadcasting Corporation) in 1988*

*Angus & Robertson Publishers
Unit 4, Eden Park, 31 Waterloo Road,
North Ryde, NSW 2113; and
ABC Enterprises
Australian Broadcasting Corporation
20 Atchison Street, Crows Nest, NSW 2065,*

Copyright © Australian Broadcasting Corporation, 1988

*National Library of Australia
Cataloguing-in-publication data.*

Downes, Jim.
   A big country.
   ISBN 0 207 15896 7.
   *1. Country life – Australia.   2. Australia –
Social life and customs.   I. Australian
Broadcasting Corporation.   II. Title.
III. Title: Big country (Television
program).*
994

*Design by April Briscoe
Typeset in 12pt Bembo by Best-set Typesetters
Printed in Hong Kong*

CONTENTS

GENESIS	1
GETTING STARTED	7
MYSTERIES, MYTHS AND LEGENDS	17
The Strange Story of Five Hundred	19
The Min-Min Light	27
Tiger Country	31
The Battle of Barcaldine	37
Magoffin's Matilda	44
ECCENTRICS	59
The Man Who Had Everything	61
Doing Something Different	64
Fire and Water	68
The Rag-Tag Railway	73
There Were No Foxes in Australia	77
SURVIVORS	81
The Last Tent Show	83
Only for the Rabbits, We'd Be Buggered	88
The Drover	93
Who Was Here First, Anyway?	99
No Place for a Hermit	105
LOSERS	113
Too Much Like a Teddy	115
'I Am Going to the Gulf'	121
The Good Shepherd	130
No Life in Simpson	135
A Trade in Bodies	139
WINNERS	145
One That Got Away	147
Truchanas	155
The Kid Who Failed Sunday School	163
Lights in the Valley	167
Taking On the System	173
FACES, PLACES	181
The Princess and the Canecutter	183
The Smartest Man on Darnley	189
It Was All Right on the Night	193
A Wedding in Katherine	197
'I've Photographed a Million Women'	203
The Golden World	206

FAMILIES	213
All Right for Some	215
Henderson's Daughters	220
Survival of the Toughest	226
Pioneering the Present	232
Gulf Battlers	238
TRENDS	245
Standing in a Dust Storm Tearing Up Money	247
Hydrogen, Carbon and Sweat	255
You Can't Carve the Silence	260
AN ACCOUNTING	265
To Measure the Past, Use the Right Clock	267
It's Nice that You Don't Know the Future	274
THE TRACK BEHIND, THE TRACK AHEAD	282

MIKE GORMAN

TIMOR
TORRES STRAIT
Darnley Island
Murray Islands
PAPUA
NEW GUINEA
TIMOR
SEA
DARWIN
ARNHEM
LAND
GULF OF
CARPENTARIA
CAPE
YORK
STRATHGORDON
CORAL
SEA
Katherine
Wyndham
Bullo River
THE
KIMBERLEYS
INDIAN
OCEAN
Broome
Halls Creek
Cairns
Normanton
Bedarra Island
YELDHAM
Ingham
Townsville
Charters Towers
NORTHERN
TERRITORY
Dajarra
Kynuna
DAGWORTH
Winton
Boulia
Longreach
Barcaldine
Alice Springs
Rockhampton
WESTERN
AUSTRALIA
MAYFIELD
QUEENSLAND
Fraser I
Maryborough
Creek
Cooper
SOUTH
AUSTRALIA
BRISBANE
Clarence
Gold
Coast
Texas
River
Dorrigo
Bellingen
Hawker
NEW SOUTH WALES
PERTH
Katoomba
SYDNEY
Port
Lincoln
ADELAIDE
Mildura
Hay
Balranald
Gundaroo
CANBERRA
Murchison
VICTORIA
Maryborough
MELBOURNE
Geelong
Simpson
SOUTHERN
OCEAN
TASMANIA
Miena
Ross
HOBART

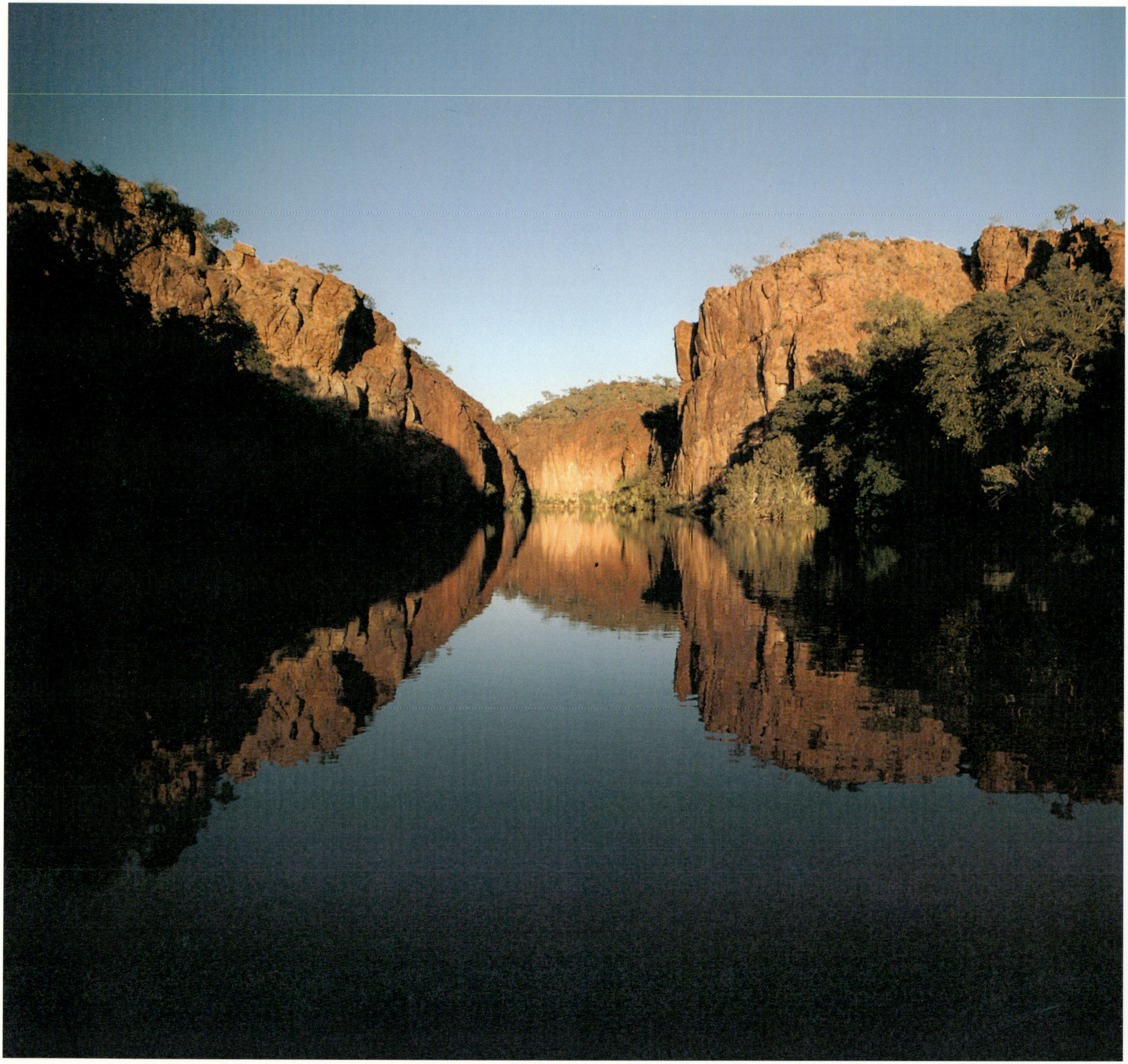

Genesis

We don't think of Australia in the emotional language of the old world: seldom do we call it The Homeland, never The Motherland or The Fatherland. And we don't often think of it as an island. Sure, the knowledge of that reality is there all right, those of us educated before they stopped teaching useful things learned by heart that what we lived on might be the world's smallest continent, but, by God, it was the biggest island. And wasn't it big: snow on the mountains at one end and crocodiles in tropical rivers at the other. Islands, as we all know in this age of cruise ships, are much smaller things you find out in the Pacific or up there somewhere in Asia. Places you go on holiday.

The poets, our poets, had words for Australia. We learned them at school, too, and quickly forgot them as adults because they were somehow embarrassingly overstated, over the top: the Sunburnt Country, the Wide Brown Land and the rest. Regardless of what we thought of it, how privately fond or proud even we might have been of it, these emotions we kept to ourselves, among ourselves. Just occasionally, these repressions might surface in outbursts of outrageous chauvinism in the presence of those we considered the less fortunate residents of other, older, distant places. But as more of us travelled, we grew out of that boastfulness. Having seen some of the world, we came more quietly, gratefully, home to what we knew.

What we knew were the cities in which most of us lived, cities situated, in the main, on that strip of the southern and eastern

Highlands water on the way to the sea: Dorrigo Plateau, NSW.

OPPOSITE PAGE: *Morning in Middle Gorge. Rarely is there water to reflect outback Australia but north-west Queensland's Lawn Hill Gorge is a spectacular exception. It's part of Lawn Hill National Park in Queensland–Northern Territory border country.* KATHIE ATKINSON

▲ A BIG COUNTRY

coasts which is the only consistently populated part of the smallest continent/ biggest island. To these south-easterners, the land that began on the other side of the Dividing Range was rarely seen, if ever, and then only in glimpses from the window of a fast-moving car or slower-moving train on the way from one city to another. Of the people who lived inland we knew little: they were the figures on red tractors at the pointed ends of the clouds of dust that we understood to be part of the ritual of farming. They were all extremely rich, we knew, because that was part of the national folklore, which also told us that out there you found the Real Australia, the Backbone of the Country, the Source of All Wealth before the diggers of holes moved in and stole both the slogan and the image. And it was all true. Somehow those grubby sheep yielded the miracle of wool, and the browning paddocks, come December, became the wheat to feed what we all knew was a great hungry world. According to season, there were rich, rolling, green paddocks or rich, rolling, brown ones and, either way, they meant food and wealth.

There were rivers and huge dams. They were blue. The mountains were blue, the colour of distant gum trees breathing. And always, for practically all of us, there was the close-by sea, dominant in our lifestyle and blue as the sky. We lived in a national, natural decor of blues and greens.

It took the space age to show us our island as it really is: dry, mostly; bare, mainly. Not blue-green at all, but red-brown. The fertile coastal fringe, the bit we most use, live on and live from, is all but invisible from space, so narrow between the oceans and the dry interior that an orbiting camera cannot distinguish it.

But at least there was proof that we were the shape we'd always been taught. Full marks, Bass and Flinders, to have drawn it all from sea level in that celebrated circumnavigation and to have got it all so remarkably right. That much we saw in those first pictures from space, reconstituted from numbers sent back to earth by the process called telemetry and needing often a touch up by an artist to ink in a more definite outline than a robot in space could provide.

Then the space men went up and walked outside their ships, Hasselblads in hand, and brought back pictures of our world as we'd never seen it before: this lovely planet, a living ball of colour in black space, and on its surface, in pictures of superb definition, this island, Australia.

But it was not our image of Australia.

Where were those food and fabric factories? Where the lush tropics, rainforests, cane fields and, to the south, the white of snow, the brown of wheat and the green of pasture? Beaches? Blue Mountains? What we saw, through the eyes of men in space, was a dry, red island, and there began to emerge a new awareness of the nature of Australia: a series of vast deserts stretched from ocean to ocean. There was no visible water between sea and sea. No green. No sign of cities, towns, farms or regions. Just A Big Country.

It was an inspired name for a television program about Australia: *A Big Country*. The title said it all, declared the parameters of the show and its purpose, defined its character and the breadth of its workplace. A program about a nation on the go, confident beyond the point of simple brashness, prosperous to a standard unimaginable even a few years earlier, assured and optimistic to a degree acceptable, near compulsory, even, at the time, but naive, deluded and deceived in hindsight.

And, like so much of the Australian society that had emerged since World War II, that program title was borrowed: it came not from the bush, from the Big Country itself, but from a B grade Hollywood movie, *The Big Country*. 'The' became 'A', presumably to avoid the possibility of litigation. And the program was conceived, planned, developed, financed and launched again not from the bush but from chaotic offices in big city buildings the ABC of the time seemed to favour.

A television program, any television program, starts as a concept, an idea in the vision of an individual or a group. The men who planned *A Big Country* knew well they had two major obstacles to cross before the idea could become a program. These were the increasingly inert bureaucracy of the ABC and a secondary bureaucracy within a bureaucracy of the Rural Broadcasts Department.

But, perversely, from an environment which should produce dedicated bureaucrats and very little else, the ABC conjures program-makers who produce collectively most of the original ideas in Australian television. Such ideas are unusual in this Australian industry. Its ideas more commonly come from a once-a-year executive-suite pilgrimage to California.

Unusual, too, that the Rural Department should produce original ideas in television, for Rural was possibly the most inward-looking of all the departments of this deeply divided organisation. Its origins lay in the various State Agriculture Departments which provided so much of its program material and so many of its people, for recruiters from the ABC and the Agriculture Departments vied to sign on each year's crop of graduates from the several agricultural colleges in the country. A diploma in agriculture was the ticket to the doors of both, and not infrequently recruits to one organisation or the other changed their minds in early career and sought the revolving door between public service agriculture and public service broadcasting.

Generally, the door revolved in one direction. The traffic favoured broadcasting, because the local and regional radio services which were the power base of the Rural Department made local celebrities of the rural broadcasters in a way that advising on agronomy or animal husbandry could not. So some very bright young men were recruited to ABC Rural. Being both talented and ambitious, some of them saw the prospect of Life beyond the *Country Breakfast Session* and beyond even the fame of the national *Country Hour*, and so one of the dangers of television quickly became apparent to ABC bureaucrats: television attracted bright and unconventional people who sought to change dull and conventional administrations. The Rural Department, long known to and denigrated by those at the smarter end of broadcasting as 'The Prograaam for the Maaan on the Laaand Baaaa!' found itself employing people whose ideas for its television future ranged far beyond the traditional advice on how to grow good things and stop the growth of bad things.

These were men who knew the bush, who mostly had come from the bush, who knew that out there in the great redness of inland Australia there were people who'd made a lifestyle that was unique, independent of trend and fashion, and the stories of their lives and works hadn't been told since the days of the bush poets. Even the *Bulletin* had deserted the bush to become a city newsmagazine. The bush needed television, and television, awash with fictional tales of other people's culture or lack of it, needed the bush. Television found *A Big Country*.

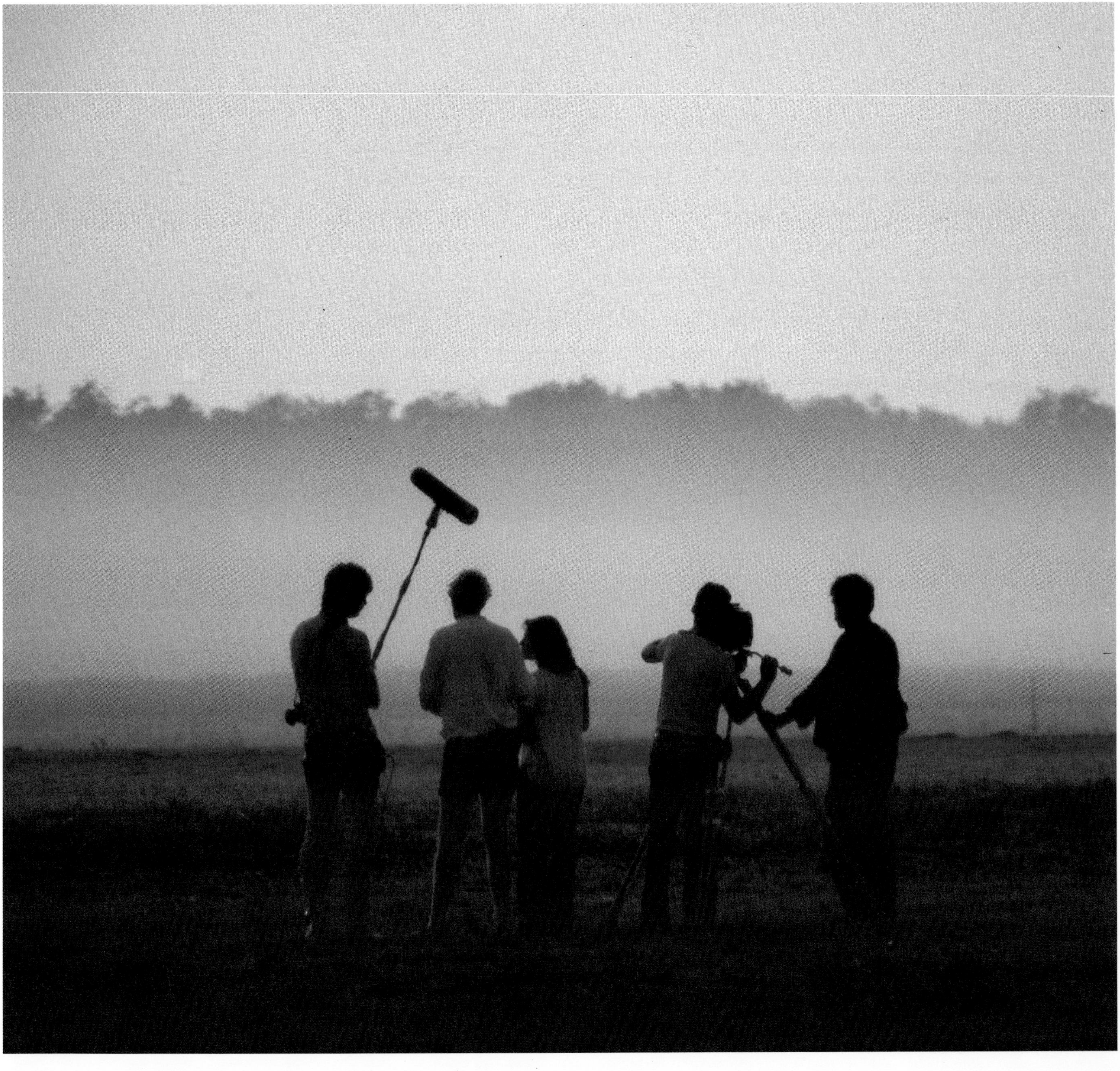

In living black and white—colour was yet seven years off—ABC Program No N3524 went on television nationally at twenty minutes past nine on the night of 5 September 1968. The presenter, the late Cam Tucker, introduced the new program and talked about the things it hoped to do. He didn't tell the audience that the program was in trouble already with the ABC bean counters: it had cost twice the allocated budget of $1200, and although by any standard half an hour of film on television for $2360 was an exercise in teleconomics, budgets were sacred. Nor did he mention that there probably wasn't much future for the program anyway, because from the very area that had created it there was building an undercurrent of opposition. The divisions between television and radio, between the old guard and the new talent, between the radio broadcasters who saw themselves with no role beyond the farmers' friend and the television program men with big ideas, these deep divisions threatened to make *A Big Country* the shortest series ever, a series of one.

The morning after the first program went to air, the ABC's Boys in the Bush, the Regional Rural broadcasters, and some of their city colleagues launched into a chorus of complaint. The program was about an emerging problem in the bush, one that has since reached huge proportions, and it told the stories of people forced off the land by the new economic wisdom, Get Big or Get Out. It was the sermon of false prophets, some would say now, but pushed hard at the time by those who saw personal advantage in it, the line had

Getting Started

GULF COUNTRY, QUEENSLAND.

OPPOSITE PAGE: 'EARLY RISING IN THE HALF-LIGHT, WHEN THE MORN CAME, BLEAK AND CHILL...'

WRITTEN LONG BEFORE TELEVISION, JOHN O'BRIEN'S LINES FROM 'THE OLD BUSH SCHOOL' DESCRIBE EXACTLY THE DISCOMFORT OF FILM CREWS SEEKING THE MORNING MAGIC OF THE BUSH.
KATHIE ATKINSON

achieved a level of belief in the bush. People were selling up. People were weighing the alternatives: borrow to become big, or sell up and go. Almost unanimously, they wanted to stay on their land in the only way of life they knew. Over and over, in interviews with troubled people, the producer, John Mabey, heard the lament which became the title of the first program, 'We Don't Want to Leave'.

To the program's opponents within the ABC, this wasn't at all the sort of thing the ABC should be doing. For the Rural Department to be doing it smacked of betrayal of Rural's traditional bush constituency. The proper role for rural was the adaptation to television of what was called 'extension', information for farmers by other farmers or by experts. What the critics had in mind, it seemed, was the *Country Hour* with pictures, television programs larded with farmspeak: broad acres, virgin land, scrub clearing, irrigation, marginal soils and (this being Australia of the 1960s) subsidies.

Their protests landed on the desks of the Mighty at Sydney head office, where sympathies historically went to the old, the comfortable and controllable when confronted by the new and troublesome. The handful of people involved in *A Big Country* were battered into near submission. Then they found a powerful Friend at Court.

Graham White had been a rural broadcaster. Now he was an executive on the move. White declined to join the pack baying for the blood of the new program. He chose instead to see what the audience thought of it. That, in those days, was a revolutionary approach for a senior ABC executive to take. White found that as internal sectional criticism mounted, the reaction of the customers, the viewers, was dramatically opposite: they liked it. Just about everyone asked for an opinion said it was good and there should be more of it. Graham White went in to bat with management, and *A Big Country* lived.

The program team had some tricks of their own: they knew well the inertia of the ABC, the huge difficulty of getting something moving. But they knew, too, that inertia could work both ways and, once started, ABC projects tended to roll on regardless. So they contrived for the program a publicity statement which described *A Big Country* as 'An ABC public affairs series on subjects outside the big cities'.

That was a master stroke: it established there would be a series; it cleared the way for the program to tackle any subject it chose; it protected *A Big Country* utterly from the territorial claims of other program departments and created a territorial claim of its own; and it scraped off the lingering traces of the farmyard. Before it was halfway through its first series, *A Big Country* had the shape that would carry it for series after series through two decades, and it had a simple winning brief declared by executive producer John Sparkes: find good stories, and tell them well. In pursuit of that, film crews in lumbering four-wheel-drives began weaving across Australia a pattern of tracks which would form a unique tapestry of the essence of Australia.

The Australia that *A Big Country* set out to cover in 1968 was having it good. But the world outside was in its customary turmoil.

Australia was learning there was life after Menzies, but that the form of political stability which could keep one Prime Minister in office for sixteen years might be a thing of the past. Holt had come, and had gone into the ocean at Portsea. National leadership was up for grabs: John Gorton was in the chair when the music stopped. He was perceived to be 'more Australian' than the others, and he promised Australian solutions to Australian problems. Problems there were, but the solutions had yet to arrive when Gorton fell from favour and an internecine struggle cost him his lease of The Lodge.

The Vietnam war, in which Australia had vastly increased its participation, had divided the country more deeply than any issue of the generation. Famed as a nation of gamblers though we may be, many Australians were outraged at the use of a lottery draw to select the eighteen-year-olds who would be conscripted and sent as soldiers to a war which half Australia considered was none of our business. It was the living-room war that came into our homes nightly at seven on the news and, for the first time, people saw a war as it happened: yesterday's battle was tonight's news. No war had been reported by television so completely before and, as a media event, the war was a huge success. There were times, watching the coverage, when it seemed the whole thing was designed for the media, kept going because there wasn't much else of interest going on at the time to fill the news. But the depth and style of the coverage, the deep scepticism of the reporters, the graphic truth of the cinecamera, combined to defeat the propaganda which had characterised previous military excursions.

Two and a bit years into the decimal age, we'd got used to dealing in dollars and cents, and the initial rip-offs had become too well known to work any more. One dollar ninety-nine replaced nineteen shillings and eleven pence as the commercial psychologists' ruse to make us think something was costing less than it really was. We financed decimally, but still weighed and measured imperially, while in Canberra an elderly and little known senator was planning his life's great work: The Metric Conversion of Australia.

It was fitting that we were going to ditch imperial standards, because the imperial system to which we'd shown such devotion for so long was showing us in certain terms that times were changing. After 180 years of imperial come-on, we were getting the imperial brush-off. The Common Market, we thought, was very common indeed, and the thought of our Mother, England, in bed with the rascally Europeans whom twice this century we'd helped her to resist made us doubt the value of all we had learned as children about the Bonds of Empire. Mother England had taken her European lovers two years before, and the seers of Australian agriculture were muttering about problems in the future. But Japan had already replaced the United Kingdom as our principal trading partner, and those fabulous holes in the ground had begun to yield their treasures of metals and energy, the once only crops that would guarantee our future.

The easy killings from minerals, though, would not be made by gnarled prospectors and hard-working miners. The quick money would go to the entrepreneurs who seldom ventured beyond the stock exchanges and their surrounding restaurants, and in 1968 the wide boys of business were sharpening their wits and their pencils, laying the baits, setting the traps, forming the two-dollar companies whose shares would trade at huge profits on the basis of nothing more substantial than rumour.

Mining, we were told, would kiss us better if things got tough for rural exports. But for every man employed digging holes, it seemed, there were two back in the big cities registering companies. In the hard red earth of Western Australia, a new national flag appeared: plastic streamers fluttering from pegs marking a mining claim. They were profitable, those pegs, and a lot cheaper than actually mining: Contract claim peggers were employed, their telegraphed in-

▲ A BIG COUNTRY

OPPOSITE PAGE:
MOUNTAINS OF IRON—THE PILBARA, WESTERN AUSTRALIA.
AUSTRALIAN PICTURE LIBRARY

structions requiring them just to peg a given number of claims in a general geographic area. Just to be near the high-fliers was enough and companies were formed, shares sold, fortunes made, on no more substantial a basis than four pegs in the earth in the Kambalda area, or near Poseidon, or close to Laverton.

Few of these claims ever felt the geologist's hammer, let alone the miner's pick. They were never intended to. In the mining business of Australia, *circa* 1968, the pen was mightier than any sward. What was mined was money. No great investment needed in machinery and people, the tools existed in any rented office and greed and gullibility brought the punters flocking in. The newspapers picked up the scent and ran with the news of a mineral bonanza, reporting the thoughts and wisdoms of a new crop of overnight millionaires. They had little to say about the losers.

'Sixty-eight was a drought year in Australia. The cotton crop on the Ord River in Western Australia had failed—again—and that costly piece of pork-barrelling was finally acknowledged to be a loser. In Queensland, a new Premier came to power, a farmer-cum-businessman with the unpronounceable, and foreign-sounding name of Johannes Bjelke-Petersen. It was pronounced 'Bee-ol-ka' we were told, and 'Jelkie' it quickly became, then, with fame, just 'Joh'.

Gold was forty-five dollars an ounce (about thirty grams), on a firmly controlled market. The bank rate went up, to 7.5 per cent, and while the national wage went up one dollar thirty-five a week, the politicians got a twenty-five per cent pay rise.

Famine struck Africa. The name Biafra joined the world rollcall of misery while, in America, the spending of untold billions of dollars sent three men to the moon and back. They flew ten times round, but didn't land: the 'Giant Step For

GETTING STARTED ▲

Mankind' was a year in the future.

The Russians invaded Czechoslovakia. Richard Nixon captured the White House and a man named Spiro Agnew achieved the second highest post in the most powerful nation on earth. Enoch Powell launched his attacks on black immigration in England. Harold Wilson's government promised an economic miracle to restore British prestige, power and prosperity.

A provincial Australian politician decided how to deal with anti-Vietnam-war demonstrators: 'Run over the bastards,' said Robert Askin. An obscure assassin in the United States decided how to deal with a politician: Robert Kennedy was shot dead, and the last credible trace of Camelot-on-Potomac was gone.

De Gaulle was President of France. Gay was a word used to describe a mood or a social event. The western monetary system was twice threatened with collapse, but tottered on. Sydney Opera House was re-costed at eighty-five million dollars. And not a penny more, they promised. They kept the promise, too, for the penny was no longer legal currency, and the promise said nothing about the thirty or forty million more dollars the Stately Pleasure Dome would absorb to complete its transformation from a tram terminus.

In Queensland, the last gangs of canecutters were being paid off, replaced by machines. And on the Australian waterfront, another labour tradition was ending. Great metal boxes called containers were bringing the first real change in 200 years to loading and unloading ships, and the wharfies' role would diminish and change forever.

Ships were changing, too. The last generation of great ocean liners had already been built, and as one by one they were scrapped during the next two decades, no new ships were there to replace them. By 1968, the line voyages which had taken generations of young Australians on the almost obligatory visit to England and The Continent were almost gone, and in the biggest factory building in the world, in Everett, Washington, USA, the Boeing Airplane Company was building the prototype of a gigantic flying machine that would revolutionise world travel, the 747, the Jumbo.

The Holden Kingswood was the Great Australian Travel Machine, one could be yours for around $3000. The petrol to drive it, sold in gallons, was the equivalent of less than ten cents a litre.

In 1968, at a hospital in Sydney, a team of surgeons performed Australia's first heart transplant; near Kalgoorlie, Western Australia, the last piece of track was laid in the trans-continental standard-gauge railway; and Australia took delivery of its first guided-missile firing warship, the destroyer *Perth*.

Yet in this same Australia, in 1968, land was being cleared for the first time, new settlers were facing the problems settlers had faced on this island since the first Europeans came. The society which this television program *A Big Country* was setting out to report, while considering itself egalitarian and homogeneous, was as diverse as a program-maker could wish for. By trading on people's natural interest in and curiosity about other people, by finding storytellers who could first find, then tell, good stories, *A Big Country* staked a claim of its own, and set about mining the rich fields of Australia: its People and Places, Heroes and Faces, Winners and Losers, Families and Failures, Eccentrics, Anachronisms, Mysteries, Myths and Legends.

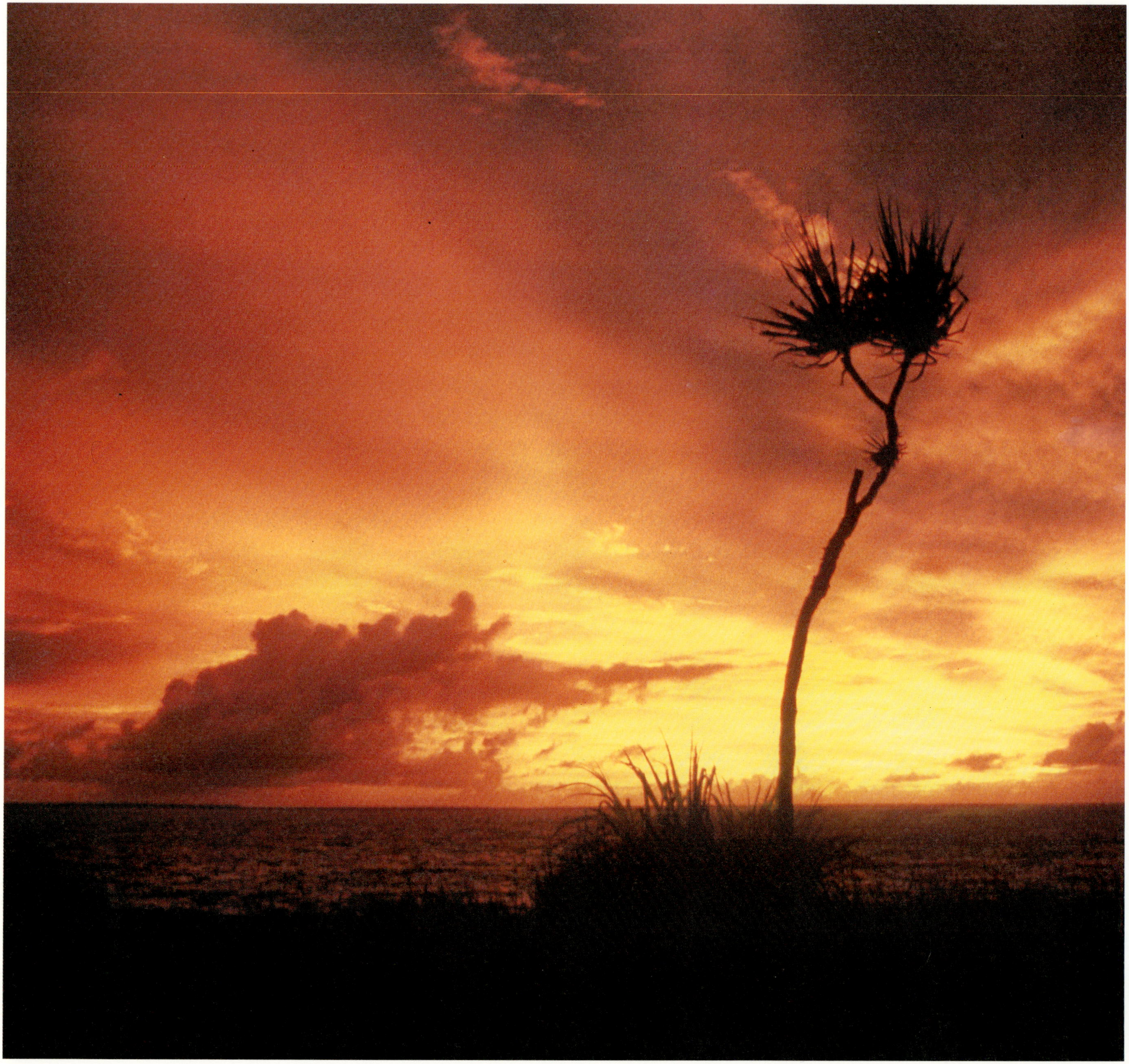

MYSTERIES, MYTHS AND LEGENDS

A MYTHOLOGY does not need millennia to develop: given enough inventive minds with a lot of spare time, a couple of hundred years is enough for a healthy collection. Australia is proof of that.

They were sometimes self-deceit, those myths of ours, and revealed as such sooner or later when better sportsmen, faster horses, braver—or more successful—soldiers, and cheaper coal mines emerged in foreign places. Twenty years on in A Big Country, *the myth of supremacy had been particularly savaged by realities.*

We were lacking in monsters, too, so we had to invent some. The unimaginable Yowie, for example, and strange lights in the western Queensland sky.

Legends came more easily: Captain Cook, the First Fleet, the chain gangs, the gold rush, the Eureka Stockade, the swagman who sank into immortality through a bush ballad that came damn close to being the national anthem.

And mysteries? The whole place was a mystery to the Europeans who had to make a home of it. They didn't know, and didn't want to know, that there'd been mysteries, myths and legends on this island for 40 000 years or more as other settlers invented stories to explain the inexplicable. But from one day in January 1788, those thousands of years of myth and legend were to be disregarded. European man had no place for them—he was bearer of his own legends, believer in his own myths, creator of altogether new mysteries.

OPPOSITE PAGE:
SUNSET IN THE TOP END. KATHIE ATKINSON

The Strange Story of Five Hundred

It is the border between daylight and dark, the twilight, a good time for mysteries. It is cold, bleak winter in eastern Victoria. The mists flow down a tree-covered mountainside. The music is eerie: television is telling us something is going to happen.

A preposterous animal with shining yellow eyes hauls itself out of the ground. No, no, it's only a tractor, making a mysterious emergence from a dark and sinister background. But what is a tractor doing in this bleak landscape, its feeble headlights fighting the weak light of a cold, white moon? Television is preparing us to be frightened.

But we'll not be frightened, will we, because just a few frames of film later we see that it's a perfectly normal tractor, being driven by what appears to be a perfectly ordinary farmer. Do not be deceived. Television is preparing us for the spectacular proof, in the following thirty minutes, that this twilight tractor driver is anything but a perfectly ordinary farmer.

He's spraying his paddock after lights out. So he's had a long day. Oh no! He's waited for this time. The moon's right, you see, and some planets are in propitious positions. But it's still nothing more sinister than spraying a paddock.

Spraying it with what?

Spraying it with witchcraft, that's what: spraying eye of newt and tongue of toad. Well, not quite. But the origin and history of the solution being sprayed by mysterious twilight on the paddocks of this Victorian dairy farm is the stuff television is made of.

ALEX DE PODOLINSKI

▲ A BIG COUNTRY

OPPOSITE PAGE: *Gathered from meatworks across eastern Victoria, cows' horns are prepared for their role in the mystery processing of cowpats into the substance de Podolinski calls Five Hundred.*

It must be, for this film on the biodynamic farming techniques and beliefs of Mr Alex de Podolinski is the most popular program *A Big Country* has ever presented. It draws 2000 letters and they keep coming in a year after the program is televised. De Podolinski gets a further 5000 letters direct. And he answers them, because he believes he possesses a unique knowledge, and he wants very much to pass it on.

This knowledge is not his alone, nor did it originate with him. De Podolinski, a man of Russian ancestry, grew up in Germany and he was one of a group of German farmers influenced in the 1920s by the Austrian philosopher Rudolf Steiner. Steiner believed he had discovered a life force concealed in the droppings of cows that, with proper processing, could bring benefits undreamed of to farming. Steiner explained his processing method and the story grew stranger and stranger: his technique required that cow manure be placed in the horns of dead cows and buried in exact ways at precise times of year. When dug up, it was no longer cow manure but a sweet-smelling, doughy substance Steiner called 'Five Hundred'. Used in only tiny quantities, this substance, Steiner taught, would leave no need for chemical fertilisers, would restore soil damaged by overuse and excessive chemical applications and would preserve what he called 'the harmony of nature'. In Alex de Podolinski, Steiner found a convert, and when de Podolinski left Europe for Australia in 1947, with him came the knowledge and the determination to test it in a new country.

Why then, had we not heard of it before, if for forty years a number of farmers had been experimenting with the Steiner method, called by now biodynamic farming? De Podolinski's ideas had got around, not widely, but enough to make a claimed total of more than 400 000 hectares being farmed by his methods. *A Big Country* had heard of the Steiner theories and had come across a

MYSTERIES, MYTHS AND LEGENDS ▲

▲ A BIG COUNTRY

OPPOSITE PAGE, LEFT: *ALEX DE PODOLINSKI RECOVERS SOME OF THE THOUSANDS OF HORNS HE'S BURIED AND* **(RIGHT)** *EXTRACTS FROM THEM A MATERIAL QUITE UNLIKE THE COW DUNG HE'D PACKED INTO THEM.*

land preparation job recognisable as Steiner technique. The landowner didn't want to talk about it on television but he put *A Big Country* in touch with de Podolinski. So began the process of convincing this modest and retiring man that *A Big Country* could be trusted to tell his story.

The story that emerged tried the credulity of everyone who worked on the program.

> *If I'm ever not in a good mood in the mornings, I very soon am once I get near the cows. They tell me exactly what I'm like. They notice cosmic happenings. A cow relates to the whole environment. To live in harmony with your environment requires a purity that's like the purity of a child. They live in the total environment. Not just on the paddock on the farm, but far further reaching. They can teach a scientist where else to look, if he's sufficiently sensitive to them.*
>
> *The cow is steady, calm, placid, harmonious. A cosmos of nature. Her digestive system is the most refined on earth.*

But why the cows' horns as containers for the manure?

The answer pushed credulity several steps further: the cows' horns, de Podolinski was saying, were in some way what held in place the placid nature, the strength of character of cows. De-horn them and something changed. The horn was a unique vessel of nature and only when buried in horns would manure transubstantiate to that mysterious substance, Five Hundred. The same manure, buried in the same place at the same time in other containers, remained manure. That buried in horns changed smell, colour, texture, and became Five Hundred.

Farmers, more than most people, are realists, hard to convince of miracles, yet close enough to the cycle of creation to realise the huge gaps which exist in the

MYSTERIES, MYTHS AND LEGENDS ▲

scientific explanation of the nature of things. Farmers, too, are conservative and often reluctant to be first in the district to try something new. If that applies to a new strain of crop, a new brand of spray, it applies a thousand times more to being identified with something as mysterious and unknown as Steiner, de Podolinski, manure in buried horns and a magical substance named like a card game.

As *A Big Country* found, few people who were experimenting with the biodynamic system wanted their efforts known about. Thori MacDougall was an exception. He is the fifth generation of his family to work a big irrigation farm in northern Victoria and ten years ago he believed he'd be the last. The land was overworked, totally dependent on chemicals to sustain any production. He heard of Five Hundred. There was nothing to lose. At the rate of just more than an ounce to the acre (about 30 grams to 0.4 hectare), at the times and conditions and seasons judged propitious, Thori MacDougall tried 'witchcraft' where science had failed.

And it worked. Wonderfully, spectacularly, miraculously, it worked. It worked so well that prosperity returned to farmer MacDougall and he decided to invest some of that prosperity in a biodynamic experiment. He bought a neighbouring property, a big rice farm, run down and abandoned by its previous owner, and little more than bare dirt.

They said I was mad when I bought it. It wasn't the best impression that anybody could get of a property, but I knew it had its potential. One man said to me, 'I thought you'd have more brains than to buy a place like that.' But he did come back to me a couple of years ago, and he said, 'Well, I'll take back what I said. You've proved what can be done with that property.'

MYSTERIES, MYTHS AND LEGENDS ▲

Thori MacDougall's restored property is the only place in Australia where rice is grown completely naturally. Most growers use chemicals in abundance, up to twenty-three different chemicals on one crop. MacDougall uses none. Other followers of Alex de Podolinski could tell similar stories, if they would. But a lot of the more successful ones aren't talking at all. They've no need to justify their methods. Biodynamics is working for them. The theories of biodynamics are applied everywhere on their farms, because the system teaches there's not a pest, a plant disease or a soil deficiency that can't be put right by some natural ingredient. Finding the ingredients is the challenge of Alex de Podolinski's life.

TOP: *THE MYSTERIOUS SUBSTANCE FIVE HUNDRED. APPLIED TO THE SOIL IN MINUTE QUANTITIES, EXTRAORDINARY EFFECTS ARE CLAIMED TO RESULT FROM IT.*
BOTTOM: *'A UNIQUE VESSEL OF NATURE' ALEX DE PODOLINSKI CALLS THE COW'S HORN; NO OTHER CONTAINER CAN PRODUCE THE SAME RESULT. THESE HORNS ARE READY FOR USE AGAIN.*

On my farm here, for twenty-four years, nothing has been used that was bought from outside. All the growth you see is based on these preparations. This one [he pours out a white powder, fine as flour] *was quartz crystal originally. We call it Fibre 1. Being silica, it stimulates the light forces, the light metabolism, the light intake of plants. I've totally stopped ground rot in cherries by applying this spray. I can create conditions inside the plant and surrounding it so that I can stop curly leaf and ground rot without using any chemicals.*

I'm deeply concerned, responsible as a primary producer, for food production that is healthy to people. I'm equally responsible that the soils in future will be as good as mine are now, and will not all the time go downhill and need more chemical applications, deprived of life, of microbes and worms, and dependent on artificial feeding of the plants. It is vital that we actually do something about the soil in the way we farm, or I really am desperate as to our future on earth, altogether. That's what it amounts to.

The unprecedented reaction to the mystery of Five Hundred proved *A Big*

Country's audience wanted more: mainly, they wanted the mystery solved. Television has taught people that within the space of a twenty-five or fifty-minute program, a mystery will be outlined, explored and solved. But this one left them up in the air. There was no solution and the reason for that was, There Is No Solution. Alex de Podolinski and the people who follow his principles of biodynamic farming say it works, and they show successful farms to prove it. Those who say it's a nonsense, that it cannot be explained, that there's no science to support it, must attack it only with words because they've no facts to support a counter-argument. Official agriculture, scientific agriculture know about it but, as far as is known, no one official or scientific has made a serious investigation.

It is, of course, perfectly possible that men of office, men of science, have quietly done studies of their own. But if you're a scientist, and you find something that confounds practically everything you've ever been taught, for which you can offer no explanation, surely there must be a temptation to say nothing much about what you've found. And especially in the company of your colleagues, and in the learned journals, to say or write nothing at all that even indicates you've been venturing round the dangerous edges of the non-scientific.

If biodynamics is to have its day, that attitude will have to change.

The Min-Min Light

A sceptic will say of history that it is 'Lies, agreed upon'. How then to define legend and myth? In the tourist business, a legend is often a Local Lie agreed upon for profit, and myths are created in its support.

Winton, in western Queensland, makes up in history what it lacks in geography. The national airline, Qantas, started there, and a generation before that, the Australian labour movement, unionism, came out of the western shearing sheds and the great shearers' strike. Neither piece of history is going to draw the tourist hordes to a small, far out-of-the-way town in western Queensland. Winton needed a myth, a legend, of its own. It discovered the Min-Min Light.

> *We pulled up at the side of the road, and the family were in the car [the veteran western Queensland politician Bob Katter said]. We saw what we thought was a motorbike approaching, and we were waiting for it to get nearer. And it just didn't arrive. It was like a soft motorbike light, and we got a bit curious and hopped in the car and drove in the direction of the light. It just seemed to stay that far ahead of us all the time, and then gradually it disappeared. That was my sighting, but quite a few of my friends, quite reputable people, have seen the Min-Min Light.*

Indeed! In fact, in some circles in the west of Queensland, a Min-Min sighting is the minimum qualification for social acceptance. Cynics would have it that the light is some form of unknown

CASHING IN ON A LEGEND: MIN MIN COUNTRY, QUEENSLAND.

▲ A BIG COUNTRY

OPPOSITE PAGE: *The Stuff of Legends: 'A Big Country' re-creation of a Queensland stockman's story of his encounter with the Min-Min Light.*

emanation from the hospitality industry, because so many of the reported sightings over the years have occurred in close proximity to hotels.

'It was terrifying, the light,' said Ernie Bates. 'To see it coming towards you. It used to come up close and you went towards it. Well, it'd just dance away from you.'

Was he alone at the time? No. It was a group sighting. 'There were two or three girls, and a couple of men as well, who lived in this hotel.'

Despite the recurrent hotel connection, Charlie Robertson stood by Ernie Bates's story. Charlie was droving one night, back in '23, and he'd rested his mob for the night on the Boulia track: 'The light appeared just after dusk, just after the cattle got settled, and it came up towards us just like Ernie described. The cattle rushed everywhere, went over the fence, went everywhere. But it never appeared again that night.'

In more modern times, Sally Ogg had a home visit from the Min Min:

My husband and I were sleeping on the veranda because it was summer time. He'd gone to sleep and I thought I saw a car coming down our back road, so I gave him a bit of a dig and said we had visitors. And this light kept coming and it came to within about thirty yards of the house and hovered there for about ten minutes, and then just went out. It was all right while I could see it, but when it went out I was very frightened.

Could it have been a car? Definitely not, says Sally Ogg: 'It was just a light, that didn't throw a beam. It was spooky.'

'Let's see if it likes a taste of lead,' said the anonymous shearer, a Cloncurry man, when tales of the Min-Min Light were doing the rounds of the bar at Boulia.

MYSTERIES, MYTHS AND LEGENDS ▲

He press-ganged a couple of mates, loaded the old .32 rifle and took some blankets into the bush to wait for the light. Jim Cardno tells the story. After an hour or two the light appeared. Closer and closer it came to the armed men in their hiding place. But no-one was game to fire. Retreat, they decided, was the wisest course and they ran in panic back to the pub.

Again, that hotel connection: one fable of the Min Min tells of its origins in a fire which burned down the shanty at Min Min, an infamous drinking place for stockmen and drovers so notorious for crime and violence that it had its own cemetery nearby. Notorious too, for overcharging and one night, in protest, the customers rioted and burned the place to the ground. The Min-Min Light, it is said, is a spirit looking for the shanty which led to his downfall. And therein is another, kinder, explanation of the thing's affinity for licensed premises.

'I was never ever frightened of it,' Jim Cardno said. 'I used to be game, I used to try to catch it. They used to tell you you'd get fifty quid if you caught it and I said, Well, I'm going to get that fifty quid. But I never ever caught it.'

And that's just as well, because once caught, once explained, there'd be no more legend. Do the hunters of America's Big Foot, Nepal's Yeti, Scotland's Loch Ness Monster, really want to catch their quarry? Or do they rather want to keep the creatures safe in the menagerie of the mind, along with the Australian Bunyip and the Tasmanian Tiger?

Tiger Country

The inflated inner tube of a tractor tyre whirls and swings like a huge black bubble in the current of a swift mountain river. In it, vainly attempting to stabilise its erratic course downstream, sits a man. He is looking for tracks of Tigers. In Tasmania.

But there are no tigers in Tasmania, one might say, if one has a less than developed sense of the absurd. If there are any, says Jeremy Griffith, the man in the inner tube, I am going to be the first to find them.

So presented, it is a scenario the *Goon Show* would reject as too wildly improbable. But apply some definitions, and an explanation or two, and a certain logic emerges: the tractor tube, most impractical of boats, is the only thing that floats and is available hereabouts. It is cheap, and its navigator and his companion trying to keep up along the river bank are Tiger hunting on an exceedingly restricted budget of two dollars a day. The Tiger, the subject of their strong belief and the object of their uncomfortable search, is the Tasmanian Tiger, not a tiger, really, more a species of marsupial dog that hasn't been seen for half a century. Fame and local notoriety are theirs the length and breadth of Tasmania if they can prove the beast is not extinct.

There is a technique of clearing a track in the Tasmanian bush, little used in bush elsewhere, in which one falls over, rises, moves forward the distance of bush just crushed flat by the fall, then falls down again to flatten another length. The taller the explorer, the faster the progress. Slow it may be, but experts like Jeremy

FOR CHEAP TRANSPORT DOWN A WILD RIVER, A TRACTOR TYRE IS HARD TO BEAT. IT'S ALSO WET, COLD AND TOTALLY UNCONTROLLABLE.

Griffith and his colleague James Malley say it is the only way to penetrate the peculiar bush of Tasmania, which grows horizontally rather than vertically as in most other places.

The early settlers of Tasmania named the Tiger. They had other words for it, too, because it was a threat to stock and was hunted down. In the 1840s, the Van Diemen's Land Company was offering bounties for scalps. Forty years later, one landowner claimed he had lost nearly 450 sheep to Tigers, and this brought government action. A bounty of one pound a head was placed on the animal and the days were numbered for the pouched dog with a wolf's head and a striped back, *Thylacinus cynocephalus*, the biggest marsupial carnivore, an oddity in Australian wildlife.

As government had a role, through the bounty, in hunting out the animal, government has since tried twice to find the Tiger again. But government-sponsored expeditions, in 1939 and 1946, failed. Tracks and traces they reported, but no Tigers. No reported sighting since 1930 has stood up under questioning, but James Malley, a farmer, and Jeremy Griffith, zoologist, clung to the belief that somewhere in that dense horizontal bush, the striped dogs would be found again. They set up the Tasmanian Tiger Centre, encouraged people to report sightings, and set out on two dollars a day to investigate the most promising ones.

If a Tassie Tiger you should find,
(You'll know him by his striped behind)
Approach with care, be very kind,
And ask him if he'd really mind.
And before you tell of him, do stop and think:
Perhaps he'd rather stay extinct.

MYSTERIES, MYTHS AND LEGENDS ▲

The Tasmanian Tiger (illustration 5, in centre of painting), a witch's brew of an animal—head of wolf and body of dog, stripe of tiger, pouch of kangaroo—last seen around 1930. More modern sightings, in scientific opinion, should be judged in relation to proximity of nearest licensed premises.

NEVILLE W. CAYLEY

▲ A BIG COUNTRY

And well he might, for he suffered a very determined effort to send him the way of the Tasmanian Aboriginal people. In the 1920s, Hobart Zoo had thirteen living Thylacines. Many were sold to zoos overseas and, by 1933, only one remained alive in Hobart. It died a year later and the 1863 prophecy of the naturalist John Gould was realised: 'When the small island of Tasmania becomes more densely populated,' Gould wrote, 'and its primitive forests so intersected with roads from the eastern to the western coast, the numbers of this singular animal will speedily diminish. Extermination will have its full sway and it will then be recorded as an animal of the past.'

But to the searchers Griffith and Malley, reported sightings were so frequent and so believable they had to be taken seriously. It was important to know if the Tigers lived because once that was proved, action could be taken, pressures applied, to protect their habitat and allow a build-up of numbers. The encounter between civilisation and another Tasmanian oddity, the Devil, was a precedent. Zoologists knew the Tasmanian Devil was pushed to near extinction in the first decade of the twentieth century, but fifty years later had so increased its numbers that it was again a problem for sheep-owners.

The Devil was a problem, too, for people like Griffith and Malley looking for sightings of the Tiger. People often claimed a Tiger sighting when what they'd seen was a Tasmanian Devil, or a Tiger Cat, or a Native Cat or simply a domestic moggy gone wild. A tabby cat gone wild could confuse even an expert. Dr Eric Guyler, a zoology lecturer at Hobart University, had seen tabbies so big that at a quick glimpse in the bush, he'd been almost certain he'd seen a Tiger. Eric Guyler had a healthy academic mistrust of a lot of Tiger 'sightings'. 'The closer the pub the more the sightings,' he observed.

He'd long believed the Tiger population might recover, but his optimism was fading. Likewise that of the intrepid searchers, Griffith and Malley, but just one good sighting report would bring their enthusiasm flashing back. 'He's definitely there,' James Malley said. 'There's no doubt in my mind whatsoever that there's a Tiger in Tasmania.'

If there's a Tiger in Tasmania, could there also be creatures unknown and as yet unseen in the bush of mainland Australia? Rex Gilroy believed there were, and his spare time was devoted to proving it. How long, though, can a man tote camera and binoculars through silent, empty bush before his faith deserts him and he comes to think nature is not going to favour him with a glimpse of the Yowie, the Great Hairy Man, two and a half to three metres tall, 250 kilograms in weight, covered in hair and having no credible place in even the Aboriginal legends where they're supposed to be reliably reported? Or the Hawkesbury River Monster, Australia's indigenous answer to the Loch Ness Monster and even less reliably reported than Nessie.

Rex Gilroy says he's seen the Tasmanian Tiger, but not in Tasmania. Near Katoomba it was, in the Blue Mountains of New South Wales, and the sight set him off on a lifetime search to prove, just to himself, that he wasn't imagining things. 'I'll never give up the search, it's my life. I've got to go into the bush and search for these creatures, and it's become an obsession.'

In the mind menagerie of Rex Gilroy there lurk the Australian panther, a species of marsupial cat left over from the Ice Age; a form of giant monitor lizard six metres long and 3000 years extinct; and, of course, the Yowie. There are probably several words for what he does. One of them, the word Gilroy uses himself, is cryptozoology: the zoology of mystery, of the unknown. Or maybe

▲ *A BIG COUNTRY*

LEFT: *JEREMY GRIFFITH, ZOOLOGIST AND TIGER HUNTER.* RIGHT: *JAMES MALLEY, ANOTHER BELIEVER, SETS A BAIT TO CATCH A TIGER.*

just the zoology of hope. Since the tale of the Tasmanian Tiger and the life's work of Rex Gilroy were filmed by *A Big Country*, no new discoveries of wildlife have shaken the scientific world, so the search must go on. Perhaps the Tasmanian Tiger has made its decision: it would rather stay extinct. And the creatures of cryptozoology, too, have made a simple decision: if Gilroy was here, they'd rather be somewhere else.

The Battle of Barcaldine

It is blessedly rare in Australia for the system, the Government, to use the force of arms against its citizens.

Eureka everyone knows about, it's been the subject of film and television drama. Fewer know of the Battle of Barcaldine. It was fought in and around the western Queensland wool town in 1891. Thousands of people were involved, the Army brought in cannon and the new and terrifying Gatling gun, yet not one life was taken. Barcaldine brought the Queensland outback to the edge of civil war. It was a battle lost, but a war won and a legend launched. It was the beginning of unionism in Australia, the end of acceptance of the way things were, and the conception of a new force in Australian politics, the Labor Party.

In the middle of 1982 *A Big Country* sent a film crew to Barcaldine to tell the story of an ambitious local dramatic effort, a play, a tableau the town was mounting to commemorate its past. What the visitors found was a town transformed, a people united, a re-creation of history on a scale seldom attempted before anywhere in Australia, and certainly not in a small, isolated town like Barcaldine. But the town had a good story to tell, one of the best stories in Australian history, and it was determined to tell it well.

Barcaldine, 1891: centre of a few people and a million sheep. The wool had grown long, it was time to shear, and on the stations of the west the pastoralists prepared for another shearing season like the ones that had gone before. Shearers' quarters were prepared, such as they were, and provisions laid in at rates per man unchanged

HISTORY AS THEATRE: CAST MEMBERS, BATTLE OF BARCALDINE RE-ENACTMENT.

▲ A BIG COUNTRY

OPPOSITE PAGE: *Day's end on a sheep station in Western Queensland.*

since the convict days: sugar and tea, eight pounds (three and a half kilograms) of flour, ten pounds (four and a half kilograms) of meat, the rations set for the chain gangs of the previous century.

No longer good enough, the shearers said of convict era rations. No longer good enough to fish the dead animals out of the drinking water tanks. No longer good enough to accept whatever pay rates the pastoralists offered. It was time to make a stand and at Barcaldine in 1891 the shearers walked out of the sheds.

It was revolt. It was revolution. It was the first united challenge to the power and authority of the squattocracy, the Bunyip Aristocracy of the Australian bush. The pastoralists appealed to their friends in Government, and Government sent police and soldiers in a panicky overreaction that threatened the peace of the west. There were mass arrests of men who had done no more than talk in groups in the streets of Blackall. They were chained together and transported to Charleville for trial and imprisonment. The unfamiliar sight of uniformed and helmeted soldiers in the dusty streets of the little Queensland sheep towns failed to achieve the effect the politicians and the graziers hoped for. Utterly uncowed, the strikers instead were enraged. They set up a camp outside Barcaldine and, in orderly rows of tents, established a financial and management structure to see them through a long strike. Discontent and frustration building for fifteen years would simmer no longer. The rage boiled over.

Inevitably, they set up their union and embraced it as fervently as a religion. The pastoralists, further outraged at this challenge to their future authority, brought in scab labour from the depressed cities of the south. There were brawls and confrontations, strikers against scabs, strikers against police and military. Shearing sheds were burned down. Yet still the pastoralists imported scab labour

MYSTERIES, MYTHS AND LEGENDS ▲

▲   *A BIG COUNTRY*

On the track between sheds, Barcaldine re-enactment.

opposite: *Architects in the eighties are finding what pioneers knew a hundred years ago—the value and versatility of corrugated iron. 'Some good trees and a ton of tin and a man can build anything. Tools? A spirit level and a crow-bar.'*

from the cities and still, somehow, the sheep were shorn.

The strike lasted six months, the shearers in their camp at Barcaldine refusing to back down on their demands for a new deal, the pastoralists, and the managers acting for absentee landowners overseas, refusing to yield an inch or a penny. The chance of settlement was not improved by the inability of each side to talk to the other: a gulf, social and economic, of historic proportions divided worker and management. They had never talked. It just wasn't done. If the manager had to speak to anyone, it was to the overseer who would pass the word down. Managers traditionally dressed in suit, hat and tie, winter and summer, and drove round the property in buggy and pair with a buggy boy along to open the gates. It was a grand life for the squattocracy. Costs were low, profits high, and a rebellious workforce was a threat to both. By the use and abuse of every power the society of the day offered them, the pastoralists fought the strikers and the dreaded union. Because even then they could see that the union could and would end their age of privilege.

Six months after the strike began, the shearers were starved back to work. Their leaders had been jailed, their strike fund was near exhaustion and food was running out. The stream of hungry men from the cities could not be stopped. Sheep were still being shorn. The strike was lost, and the men went back to the sheds. But with them went a spirit they'd never had before, and an experience of the power of united action. They had a vision of the end of the age of unearned privilege and employer arrogance, and from their long and noisy meetings under the Tree of Knowledge at Barcaldine there would come eventually a new and different society.

In the Barcaldine of 1891 there was hardly a family or an individual un-

MYSTERIES, MYTHS AND LEGENDS ▲

▲ *A BIG COUNTRY*

MYSTERIES, MYTHS AND LEGENDS ▲

touched by the great shearers' strike. In the Barcaldine of 1982, there was hardly anyone not involved in the great re-enactment. The Queensland Government's Department of the Arts provided a professional director, Gilbert Spottiswood, and the community provided a cast of 150 with another 150 standing by as reserves. Horsemen would ride sixty kilometres into town for rehearsals and, when the time came for the performance, everyone agreed that, as a pageant, it had gone off well. But there was more to it than that. This was a community coming together to explore its past and, from the past, gaining strengths that would serve it well in the future. It was a community effort of rare value, that brought life to history and reminded people whose lives are relatively comfortable and secure that things only got that way because in Barcaldine, in 1891, some determined men demanded change.

OPPOSITE PAGE: *SUNSET MUSTER, WESTERN QUEENSLAND.*

Magoffin's Matilda

RICHARD MAGOFFIN

OPPOSITE PAGE: *MUSIC BY CHRISTINA MACPHERSON, LYRICS BY A. B. PATERSON— THE ORIGINAL SCORE AND MANUSCRIPT OF THE NATIONAL SONG.*

THE WORDS OF 'WALTZING MATILDA' REPRODUCED WITH THE PERMISSION OF RETUSA PTY LTD AND ANGUS & ROBERTSON PUBLISHERS

Have you ever heard, in a faraway place, the music of 'Waltzing Matilda'? Perhaps someone whistling, or ragged song drifting on the boozy air coming from a London pub, or the plaintive notes of an inexpertly played harmonica two compartments away fighting with the noises of a night train in Europe. Or, if you were lucky, the sheer exhilaration of a symphony orchestra or a full brass band. Orchestra to mouth organ, such is the infinite adaptability of that simple tune. And, heard in a far-off place from whatever source, it has the power to produce an emotional reaction in even the most laconic Australian. More than any of the grander tunes which lay claim to national meaning, 'Waltzing Matilda' is the Australian song.

Most people have a sketchy idea of its origins: that Banjo Paterson wrote the words, a Miss Macpherson set them to a loose old tune she found somewhere, and the whole thing came together on a sheep farm somewhere in western Queensland. All of which is true, up to a point, but the full story is much, much more, and gathering, researching, proving that full story has occupied for years the spare time of the bush balladist Richard Magoffin.

'Waltzing Matilda' has long fascinated Magoffin. He didn't think much of earlier scholarly research done on its origins and history and set out to do better. He took the bushman's approach because, though he's a teacher now, his origins were in the bush. He was a sheepman in the harsh dry west of Queensland, and would be still had it not been for defeat at the hands of drought in the 'sixties.

MYSTERIES, MYTHS AND LEGENDS ▲

▲ A BIG COUNTRY

OPPOSITE PAGE:
COMBO WATERHOLE, NEAR WINTON, QUEENSLAND, SAID TO BE THE SITE OF HOFFMEISTER'S SUICIDE AND, THEREFORE, THE SWAGMAN-HAUNTED BILLABONG OF 'WALTZING MATILDA'.
PETER KNOWLES

He left the sheep and the land his family had run for most of the century, and studied to be a teacher. From the union of bush and book came Richard Magoffin, Poet, Balladist:

The tourist, plump and well attired,
One of the city push
Came in today and he enquired
'I say, is this the bush?'
No. This is not the bush my friend.
The bush is nowhere near.
The black stump was just round the bend
But it's no longer here.
Its borderline was not defined
But it was here no doubt
Before the modes of men inclined
To move it further out . . .

There's the lilt of Paterson in much of Magoffin's writing, so it's not surprising that he's a Matilda admirer. As a native of the area, he knew the popular theory of the song's origins was right and he decried the opposing arguments. But he wanted to know more, the times, the places, the people, the circumstances and, above all, was there a swagman, was there a sheep stolen, was there a police chase, and was there a billabong suicide?

He wanted to know where the song really came from, and he sought an explanation of how the simple ballad of a swagman, an amputated section of creek called a billabong, and a stolen sheep came close to being the national anthem and,

MYSTERIES, MYTHS AND LEGENDS ▲

whether official or not, was held by a lot of people to be the national song of Australia. *A Big Country* told for the first time Richard Magoffin's full story of 'Waltzing Matilda'.

> *Several books have been written and they all got it wrong. Furthermore, they even said that Banjo Paterson didn't write the words and somebody else wrote the music. Rot! It was written here in the bush, up here in the north-west of Queensland. We knew that, and so I set about proving it and turning legend into history.*

Magoffin was just in time. Left even another year or two, his investigations couldn't have succeeded because time was overtaking his living witnesses. As it was, the events of ninety years before came second hand: 'My old dad,' the local said, 'always taught me that it was done here one night when they had a sing-song and Banjo was there, and they put it down, she put it to music to a Scottish kind of tune. That's how it was. He told me that.'

Richard Magoffin found scores of people each with a family story and a personal interpretation of events. Like a policeman investigating a traffic accident, he learned of the infinite capacity of people to interpret, embellish, personalise. Add the complication of time and the vagaries of ageing memories, and the bush detective faced an historical jigsaw puzzle with the added dimension of time.

> *There were various versions of the 'Waltzing Matilda' story alive in our district that had passed down through various families. Some were myths, some were legends, and it was necessary to find where the myth finished and the legend began. What really got me started was in 1966 somebody sent me a copy of a book written by a Melbourne author, an 'expert', and he didn't even have the song being written*

here. It was written somewhere else, by someone else, and it said Paterson didn't even write the words. It's the greatest lot of codswallop you've ever seen. He never came near the place. He sat in an office or in his home in Melbourne, went to a few libraries, but never came near the 'Waltzing Matilda' country. I thought it was time somebody got off their bot and came up and had a look at the place. None of them ever did, so it was necessary for a local bloke to set about and do it.

A. B. PATERSON, 'BANJO'

In the pub at Kynuna, Magoffin met Viv de Sailly, an old-timer who'd known the Macphersons of Dagworth Station, and with a visit to the former site of Dagworth homestead, a twenty-year detective hunt through the folklore of the west began. Magoffin used every source he could: human memory, old newspapers, even the weather records of the time and, piece by piece, the story came together.

Andrew Barton Paterson, the Banjo to us now, but Bart or Barty to his friends at the time, went to Dagworth Station with his fiancée, Sarah Riley, whose father was a district squatter. Sarah's best friend was Christina Macpherson, sister of the owner of Dagworth. It was January of 1895. A second strand enters the thread of the story: it was the time of the second shearers' strike in Queensland.

Paterson the journalist was sympathetic to the cause of the rural workers. Although he came from a land-owning family, his feelings were with the bush workers. His background meant he knew at first hand the injustices that had brought on the shearers' strike. He pressed his host for details of the armed confrontation—pitched battle might say it better—that had taken place at Dagworth four months before. Six district woolsheds had been burned to the ground, Dag-

▲ A BIG COUNTRY

OPPOSITE PAGE:
The homestead on Dagworth Station, Winton, Queensland. From its beginning here in 1895, 'Waltzing Matilda' spread nationally in a couple of years.
DOUGLASS BAGLIN

worth was to be the seventh. Squatter Macpherson called for extra police and mounted guard, and at midnight on a September night in 1894, the attack came. There was a gunfight rare in Australian history that went on for an hour or more. Someone later counted the shells: seventy shots had been fired in about twenty minutes at the pitch of battle. None hit anything other than buildings, a comment either on the marksmen or their intentions.

The latter, according to Richard Magoffin's view of history: he's convinced the orders to put the torch to the shearing sheds came from the city, from labour leaders safely removed from the scene of action and from the retribution certain to follow. Their aim was rebellion in western Queensland, the overthrow of the squattocracy and their friends in Government, and the creation of a local republic. (Remember that William Lane and his pitiful New Australia colony in Paraguay, South America, came as a direct result of the failure of the Queensland shearers' strike.)

Magoffin applies the bushman's perspective to history and believes the aim of the marksmen in the gunfight at Dagworth shearing shed was deliberately deflected by a kind of bush brotherhood, in which workers and boss were both bushmen and therefore reluctant to shoot to kill.

But in the brisk traffic of bullets, there was one determined activist who managed to set the shed on fire. Its greased boards burned like kindling, and in minutes from the striking of match on boot, the shed was doomed. With it burned 140 lambs, and that was a crime in any bushman's book. A thousand pounds was on the head of the man who struck that match. As the sun rose on the smoking ruin and the smell of burning wool and roasted flesh, Macpherson and a policeman set out to track the fleeing strikers.

MYSTERIES, MYTHS AND LEGENDS ▲

Hear the words of the song fading in? Up rode the squatter, mounted on his thoroughbred, up rode the trooper...

They caught up with their quarry at a place called Four Mile Waterhole, a group of living men and one dead man, Samuel Hoffmeister, dead of a gunshot wound. The question unanswered then and unanswered now, despite Richard Magoffin's best inquiries, is who shot Hoffmeister, and why? Was he the man ordered by planners far away to fire the shed? Was he, as his companions maintained, just a bit of a simpleton caught up in affairs beyond his grasp and moved by the heat of the moment to strike a match on his boot and burn down a shed? Did his companions, knowing pursuers were bound to catch them up, kill him before he could name names? Or did he kill himself, as the local magistrate decreed at the inquest?

This, it is safe to assume ninety years on, was the tale squatter Bob Macpherson told his house guest A B Paterson. This was the loom of fact on which Paterson, the poet, began to weave a tale assured of immortality.

Once a looney firebug, name of Sam Hoff-mei-ister...No. That's not right.

Once a nutty German, with a box of ma-hat-ches...No.

Once a happy union man, sent to do some firelighting...

Once a happy, no, jolly German man, swag upon his shoulder...

Once a Jolly Swagman...

That is the kind of process by which things are written. That is how stories are told, songs and poems created, legends brought forth. It's called poetic licence.

Richard Magoffin's singular contribution to our knowledge of ourselves and the things we hold to be important was to see for the first time a link between

MYSTERIES, MYTHS AND LEGENDS

events: to relate the burning woolshed and the death, cause unknown, of an otherwise anonymous bushman, to the social, romantic even, visit of A B Paterson to the scene soon afterwards. To link Paterson's known sympathies for the bush and its people to his abilities as a balladist and storyteller and, finally, to bring in the last thread to the fabric of his story, Miss Christina Macpherson, who possessed a knowledge of what we'd call today Folk Tunes.

Richard Magoffin believes he's located the very room in which it all came together even though, nowadays, the homestead on Dagworth Station is on a different site. It's the same building, the same timber and iron, but it's sixteen kilometres away from where it was when Paterson, his fiancée Sarah Riley and her friend Christina Macpherson started playing with words and music one night in January 1895. The reason for moving the house was the best of reasons in the dry west of Queensland: there was a better water supply at the new site. But the re-assembled house is the same as it was, the present owners of Dagworth, the Currs, have made sure of that, and they were able to show their old friend Richard Magoffin the room in which an Australian legend began.

You had to sense the spirit of the times and take yourself back there to unravel it all, [Magoffin says.] *We know who was around that table, in 1895, because there were at least twelve people here that night: Banjo, the guest of honour, and Sarah. Bob's brothers would have been over the other side, and his father...*

The fancy proceeds. But it's more than fancy. Twenty years of Richard Magoffin's life have gone into this research, and he's as confident of his facts as if he'd been the thirteenth guest at the Dagworth dining table on the night when Christina Macpherson began picking out a tune on an autoharp. The tune was an

CHRISTINA MACPHERSON
MRS DIANA BAILLIEU AND MRS JOAN McRAE

old Scottish air called 'Craigielea' she'd heard a year before while on holiday in Victoria and Christina's talent was such that a tune, once heard, was never forgotten. Note by word and word by note, the harp's strings and the poet's thoughts merged.

The station overseer, Jack Carter, a guest at the dinner table, casually reported that during his day's work he'd met a swagman 'waltzing matilda' down by the river. Paterson queried the words and someone knew it was an old German expression. In Austria and Germany, *Walz Mathilde* was an army camp follower or prostitute, and when the soldiers didn't have an actual Mathilde available, they gave the name to their greatcoats. In Australia, though, it had come to mean a light swag carried on a couple of shoulder straps. Poetically, the phrase was a godsend. Down it went, and the old air of the highlands, 'Craigielea', yielded notes to match.

At the end of that January night, in the heat of the north-western wet season of 1895, the twelve people in that dining room of a remote sheep station were unaware of the presence of a thirteenth, for he was far in the future, and his eavesdropping on their conversation would come to him second and third hand long after they were dead. They had no reason to know they'd had any more than a 'musical evening' common in the society of the time. How could they know they'd created a national legend, that people would discuss and debate the origin and meaning of their words and music a hundred years later, that a man would spend twenty years getting right the events of their pleasant evening, and that Australians nearing the turn of another century would whistle, hum, sing and be moved by their ballad of the bush.

Yet no monument marks the spot. To Richard Magoffin's anger, the original site of Dagworth, the birthplace of 'Waltzing Matilda', is not much more than a rubbish dump nowadays. It was left to some American tourists, enthused by the tale, to put up a plaque. They'd come with tuckerbag and damper from Marine City, Michigan, to stand on the bank of the billabong and sing.

Over twenty years of life with Matilda, Magoffin became absorbed, almost to the point of obsession, with the lives and personalities of the people he studied, and he learned that music to some people is more than an art; it is a business, and when people apply themselves to profiting from it, strange results can follow.

Magoffin had made something of a personal heroine of Christina Macpherson. He regarded her as a friend, as someone he knew well, though, of course, they'd never met and she'd been dead fifty years. And when he discovered that, to this day, the sheet music for 'Waltzing Matilda' sold in Australia credits the music not to Christina Macpherson but to a Sydney woman named Marie Cowan, and that to perform the song in America one must pay royalties to an American company which owns the rights, he realised his crusade was far from ended.

He'd gone as far as he could go in north-west Queensland. Ahead of him now lay first a piece of detective work, then the task of changing a business and public perception. Some dogged sleuthing produced evidence that in 1903 Banjo Paterson had taken a bundle of his unpublished work to Angus and Robertson, his publishers, and had sold them the lot for five pounds. Included were the words of 'Waltzing Matilda'

A Sydney tea merchant, James Inglis, saw the poem and, in it, an advertising opportunity. He was marketing a brand of tea called Billy. The poem, with some suitable music, was just what he needed. Was there music? He seems to have

MARIE COWAN
GEOFFREY COWAN

asked everyone except the one man who knew, Banjo Paterson himself and, convinced there was no music, Inglis asked the musically inclined wife of one of his managers to provide some. And here, the arm of coincidence is strained. Mrs Cowan's offering was almost indistinguishable from the music setting Christina Macpherson had provided at Winton eight years before. Mrs Cowan did not want to be credited as composer, her husband wrote long after her death, because she objected to the music being used in advertising. So she was, and is, described on the sheet music as arranger. Of Christina Macpherson there is no mention at all. It was Mrs Cowan's name that went with the music to World War I and Mrs Cowan's name on the documents lodged when the Melbourne music publishers Allans sold the United States rights to the work to an American company. The song is long out of royalty in Australia, but in America different laws apply and the company will go on collecting until 2011. With Australia more prominent in the United States' tourist and entertainment industries now than it's ever been, 'Waltzing Matilda' is earning a lot of dollars for her American masters.

Magoffin would challenge that. Among the findings of his long search are two original manuscripts handwritten by Christina Macpherson. At Magoffin's request, forensic scientists in the Victorian police laboratories checked handwriting on the manuscripts with writing in a Birthday Book left by Christina to a surviving grand-niece. The writings match, there can be no doubt of it, the manuscripts are the original Winton version, written by Christina eight years before the Sydney effort of Mrs Cowan. Magoffin is convinced that in those eight years, the song had spread the length and breadth of Australia—he's established it was being sung on the Murray river boats eighteen months from the time it was written at Dagworth Station, and the swagman had become a folk hero, a symbol of desperate opposition to the squattocracy. Mrs Cowan would have heard it and done pretty much the same as Christina, recalled the tune by ear and noted it down, quite unaware someone else had done the same thing.

No mention of 'Waltzing Matilda' marks the grave of Christina Macpherson. The headstone bears no inscription, not even her name. Magoffin found it on a cemetery map in Melbourne. Just Grave No 250. And that he finds saddest of all.

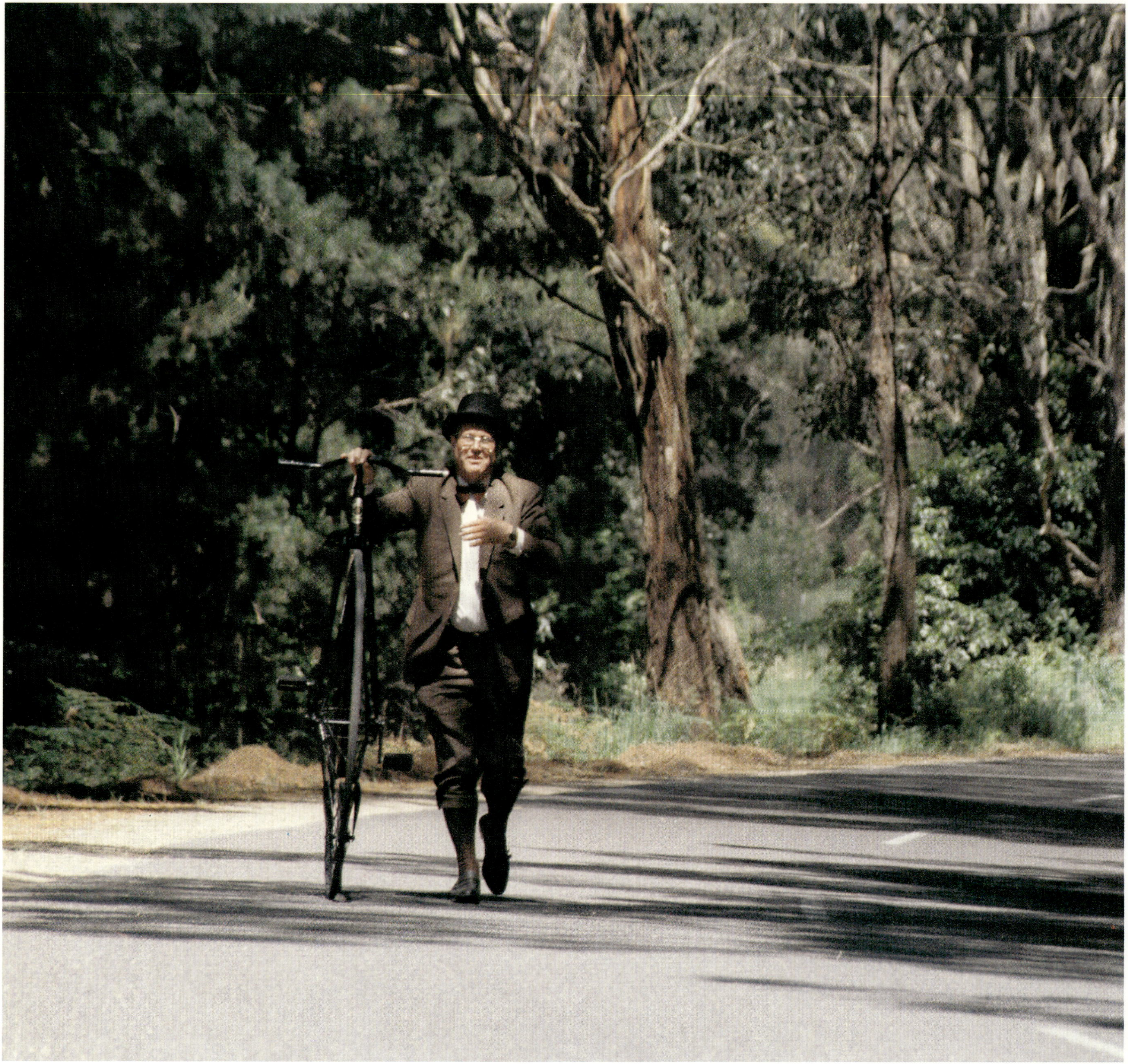

ECCENTRICS

THE WORD 'ECCENTRIC' tends to be misused in Australia, to be given a meaning which destroys the delightful essence of the word. 'Irregular, odd, whimsical', says the Pocket Oxford, but it sometimes seems that in Australia, 'eccentric' means simply 'loony'. So it is necessary to exercise some care when labelling a person, a group of people, a collection of television stories, as being 'eccentric'.

So let's rely on the Pocket Oxford's definitions 'irregular' and 'whimsical'. Together they cover a multitude of human types and human interests. Who, other than the most soulless of bureaucrats, wants a world of regular people? Who, other than the uptightest of wowsers, would disapprove of whimsy? Certainly, without the irregular and the whimsical, television would be all the poorer. A Big Country has never gone out of its way to find eccentrics, but the law of averages dictates that in twenty years of pointing cameras at this society, Australia, some eccentrics would find their way onto film. And, without exception, they would provide programs that were worthwhile and memorable. Some were people with absorbing interests. Some were people with little that was material, but deep wealth of character. One was The Man Who Had Everything.

OPPOSITE PAGE: IAN ARMSTRONG, THE COLLECTOR, RETURNS IN TRIUMPH AND FITTING FINERY FROM AN EXPEDITION WHICH HAS YIELDED ANOTHER TREASURE, A PENNY-FARTHING CYCLE.

The Man Who Had Everything

Ian Armstrong, Collector. Not Collector the village near Canberra, but collector the person, the type, the bower-bird. It is quite safe to label Ian Armstrong eccentric, because it's his description of himself: 'I think we're a fairly rare breed, although I think there are lots of people with the collector instinct built into them but quite often it ends with a stamp collection or a few bottles along a shelf or a few pictures on the walls. I've just gone a little bit further.'

A little bit further, indeed. Ian Armstrong was filmed at home, where he lived alone in a house of indescribable disorder—to the outsider. But to the collector, there was a place for everything and everything was in its place: six hundred shoe horns, for example; four to five hundred button hooks; the nation's biggest collection (possibly only collection) of Georgian shoe buckles.

As any dedicated collector knows, one thing leads inexorably to another. Ian Armstrong finds that an item bought on the spur of the garage sale, a one-of-a-kind piece with no place in any of his existing collections, will often set off a new collection, a new field of research and study.

> *Till recently I didn't realise I had a hat collection. I just used to like the odd hat here and there and I bought this and bought that and used to wear that one and when I put them all out together I realised there's a reasonably significant hat collection there.*
>
> *The pop-up opera hat, easy to stow and carry, pops up just like that. It's made by Lock & Co in London who are famous hatters in*

IAN ARMSTRONG, COLLECTOR.

▲ *A BIG COUNTRY*

ECCENTRICS ▲

St James—they've been there since the 1770s. I've got a book upstairs that tells about Lock & Co. Very famous hatters.

You collect because you like things, you like the thrill of acquiring them. It's a bit like going prospecting for gold: a win to a collector is to pick up something that really fills a gap or really is something everybody wants that only you found because you were right on the split second when it came up . . . [and he swoops with glee on the head of a Gerry Gee doll. Just the head, what use is just the head?] *Well, I've got another one and you often find these ventriloquist's dolls with broken heads, so this is at least a good head to start with to get another one complete.*

I often stand aside and look at myself as perhaps others see me, and I suppose I would see myself as an eccentric—I hope in the nicer side of the meaning of the word, a person who goes a bit against the mainstream. I'm generally doing something that's different.

OPPOSITE PAGE: IAN ARMSTRONG, AND PART OF 'A REASONABLE HAT COLLECTION'.

Doing Something Different

Mike Hayes, the Prickle Farmer.
MIKE AND JANET HAYES

OPPOSITE PAGE: *The Prickle Farm homestead. Built in 1874, it was a blacksmith's cottage until the 1920s. 'It had fallen into ramshackle disrepair when we moved in,' the owner says of it. 'But it seemed a shame to change it.'*
MIKE AND JANET HAYES

A Big Country has shown time and again that while society at large may be headed apparently in one direction, individuals or groups often head the opposite way. They choose, in the words of collector Ian Armstrong, to do something different.

Australia has a long history of movement, almost migration, of people from the bush to the cities, but the twenty-year history of *A Big Country* has seen a significant movement the other way. 'Going Bush' has an altogether different meaning for those whose parents left the bush in search of life in the cities. Their children now hanker for the bush and, to live there, they'll cheerfully accept living conditions which in the cities would bring the social workers and the charities calling to offer help.

A Big Country found journalist Mike Hayes and Janet, his wife, the main characters in the story of Emmy Lou Cabbage, Wally the Wonder Dog, Charlie Pride, Cactus Jack and the Gundaroo half-acre. If the name Mike Hayes rings only a faint bell, mention of his country estate will identify him to thousands: the Prickle Farm, he called his half-acre (0.2 hectare) lot at Gundaroo, a blink-and-you've-missed-it village outside Canberra, and the name went with him to a later rural venture elsewhere. His tales of life on the Prickle Farm were widely broadcast and printed. He's a city funny man turned bush humourist, and his tales are gently hilarious accounts of life in a rural village, Australian style.

The goat is Blossom, intelligent and rat cunning, devious, and a villain. Cactus Jack is a horse, the world's smallest, Mike says,

64

ECCENTRICS ▲

and was the unwanted prize in a trendy Canberra raffle. The sheep flock totals one, Charlie Pride, 'a wonderful, affectionate, funny creature', but who proved, after extensive scientific study, to be incredibly stupid.

There was nothing carefully planned, Mike Hayes says, about the Hayes's descent upon Gundaroo. They were living in Canberra, saw the place advertised and drove casually out to look at it.

We parked at the bottom of the lane and there were all the trendies, their Volvos snarling and engines still running, walking in, taking one look and fleeing back to Canberra. We had no money, we had no desire to live in the country. Janet said, 'What d'you reckon?' I said, 'We're bloody mad not to take it.' We bounced a cheque for the holding deposit.

Not much happens five days of the week at Gundaroo. The residents who, like the houses they occupied, were largely in original condition, saved their commercial energies for weekends when the bored residents of Canberra drove the thirty-five kilometres 'for a quick squiz at the quaint country folk'. The quaint country folk could be found seeking sanctuary from the tourist hordes in the wine bar of Matt Crowe, licensed to sell only wine because an earlier Crowe forgot to renew the full hotel licence in 1898 and no-one had since bothered to re-apply. Matt sells port, potato chips and cigarettes, the basics for life in Gundaroo, Mike says. If you want more out of country life, you can cross the bitumen road to the store where the tourists are.

For the locals, Crowe's wine bar is more than a social centre. It's where items of great moment are discussed, where tactics in the recent battle of giants in

ECCENTRICS ▲

touch football are reviewed and where Matt's body-building port is imbibed, for the sake of the health. A doctor would starve in Gundaroo, Matt Crowe says, and he takes seriously his responsibility for the health of village folk. Must be doing something right, he says, for at the last three local weddings, each of the bridegrooms was over seventy. And a tour of the headstones in the village cemetery indicates the average age at death was about ninety.

Even the cemetery bears a touch of Gundaroo humour, at the grave of one Patrick O'Shaugnessy, died at Fairfield, Gundaroo, 4 July 1844. Where a lesser man would have engraved 'Safe in the Arms of Jesus', or 'Gone to His Reward', the way Matt Crowe told it, Patrick had the stonemason carve in the granite his last protest to an uncaring world: 'I Told You I Was Sick.'

Patrick O'Shaugnessy, Matt Crowe, Mike Hayes the Prickle Farmer and the village of Gundaroo, eccentrics all, doing something different.

LEFT: TOM HAYES, THE LITTLEST PRICKLE FARMER, BRINGS HOME THE YEAR'S PUMPKIN CROP. RIGHT: CHARLIE PRIDE, THE WORLD'S FATTEST SHEEP, BABY-SITTING. MUFFETT, THE LITTLE GOAT ON HIS BACK, ISN'T AS SILLY AS SHE LOOKS; BECAUSE OF CHARLIE'S HABIT OF DUCKING IN UNDER THE PERSON FEEDING THE CHOOKS, HIS FLEECE TENDS TO HARBOUR ALL SORTS OF GASTRONOMIC DELIGHTS.
MIKE AND JANET HAYES

Fire and Water

A tractor of the steam age.

OPPOSITE PAGE: *Knock out a window, wheel up an engine and light the fire, and there's power where it's needed. Engines like this began the mechanisation of farming in Australia.*

In the 1970s, as the still prosperous Australian agricultural industries financed the purchase of bigger and ever bigger farm machines, *A Big Country* found a group of dedicated individuals moving the other way, restoring the steam-powered farm machines which had served their grandfathers and which had survived only as rusting hulks. They were too big and awkward to be disposed of in any other way. Survivors of an age when metal was metal, they were too sturdy to fall victim to the corrosion which sets upon and destroys their more modern equivalents.

Fire and water were their elements: from fire and water they made power and began the mechanisation of farming, and their age lasted until the ease and convenience of the internal combustion engine, allied with the superior marketing skills of the tractor-makers, pushed steam power into the back paddock, to gently decay.

There they were found by the steam enthusiasts, the steam freaks. Begged or bought from uninterested owners, hauled somehow to distant workshops, stripped and rebuilt, they emerged again in a finery only the enthusiast will take the time and spend the money to achieve. Priceless now, painted and polished and pampered, anointed with oil rather than merely lubricated, they're fired up and show their stuff at half a dozen or more steam fairs around the country, great flywheels turning regally, pistons and rods flashing, breathing out busy puffs of steam and the fragrance of coal smoke and hot oil.

George Johnson, demonstrating his farm traction engine,

ECCENTRICS ▲

▲ A BIG COUNTRY

BELOW: *'WE'RE OK FOR FUEL, NOW JUST FIND A DAM AND WE CAN RUN ALL DAY FOR NOTHING.' WHAT IT LACKED IN SPEED, THE STEAM LORRY MADE UP FOR IN POWER AND ECONOMY.*

OPPOSITE PAGE: *RESCUED FROM THE RUST HEAP, STEAM TRACTION ENGINES AWAIT THE ATTENTION OF STEAM ENTHUSIASTS WHO WILL SPEND WHATEVER TIME, TALENT AND MONEY NECESSARY TO RESTORE THEM TO AS NEW CONDITION.*

claimed he could be ready for work two hours after lighting the fire. That, of course, was one of the reasons steam couldn't compete: a petrol, diesel or kerosene tractor could be ready in a matter of seconds. But George Johnson, like the steam engines he loved, was a man of an age when the saving of time wasn't the fetish it later became. And, as he was quick to point out, in return for waiting that couple of hours, the operator could get power for next to nothing: 'My wood costs me nothing, I've got it on the place. My water's in the tank, runs off the roof. All it costs me is a few cents for a bit of oil.'

ECCENTRICS ▲

▲ A BIG COUNTRY

I was shearing for the fellow I bought this engine off. He said to me, 'You've got to cart water, you've got to cart wood for these things, I'm going to get a diesel.' I bought this off him and he got the diesel. He never lost half an hour with the steam engine over the whole of the time he was using it, I think something like twenty years, he bought it new from England, but the first year he had his diesel he lost a day's shearing. He didn't understand it so well, and it didn't go.

In the old days, when I was travelling shearing, we wouldn't go to a shed if it had an oil engine in it. You'd be sitting down every day for half an hour or an hour, something would go wrong and they'd have to get a neighbour or an expert to fix it. But with the steam engines we lost no time. In those big sheds we had the big twin-cylinder steam engines. Oh, beautiful things they were, driving thirty, thirty-five, forty stands. It was wonderful to work with.

The Rag-Tag Railway

Does the wonder of steam improve with memory? Would the old man who now recalls steam with such admiration and affection have roundly cursed steam machinery in his youth when he was required to fire, clean or operate it?

Perhaps, but there's no shortage of young men of the 1980s keen to work on old steam machines and, what's more, to do it for nothing or even to pay for the privilege. *A Big Country* found in the north of New South Wales one of the most significant railway preservation projects anywhere in the world, where a complete railway is under restoration by an entirely volunteer workforce. Closed down by the railways as uneconomic, the mountain line to Dorrigo one day will be an operating railway museum.

There are few railway lines in Australia so well suited for the role. It is sixty-nine kilometres from the coastal main line junction to the Dorrigo terminus, sixty-nine kilometres of constant climbing which took the little trains five hours to cover. There was plenty of time to admire the scenery, and the scenery repaid the effort because this is one of Australia's most beautiful places. The line was built in the heyday of railway expansion: 700 men worked on it for two years, and legend says it cost a pound an inch.

Once opened, the line made its own rules and regulations: it was a safe distance from management, and the locals dubbed it the Rag-Tag Railway. It ceased to be economic long before its closure —there are good reasons to doubt if it ever was an economic proposition—but economics had little to do with railways in those days.

Engine 5069, first to run on the restored Dorrigo line.

▲ A BIG COUNTRY

BELOW: *Often one step ahead of the scrap metal men, the Dorrigo enthusiasts scoured NSW for such museum pieces as this, a 100-year-old 19 class.*

OPPOSITE PAGE: *A picture of men on holiday. From city and town and farm they converge on Dorrigo to haul sleepers, bend rail, drive spikes and rebuild a railway. Their aim is a living museum of steam trains, one of the best in the world.*

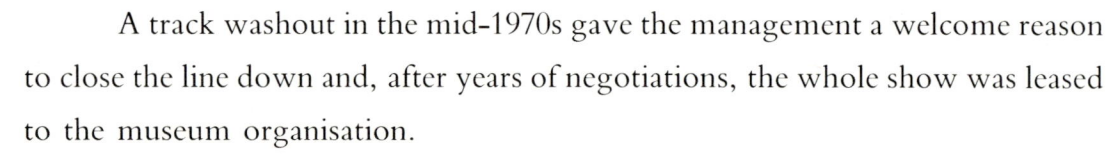

A track washout in the mid-1970s gave the management a welcome reason to close the line down and, after years of negotiations, the whole show was leased to the museum organisation.

To call the museum group an organisation is to stretch the truth of that time. It was primarily the enthusiasm of one man, Keith Jones, and a few fellow spirits he gathered about him. They had begun with the rescue of one old steam locomotive from the scrapper's yard. Then they heard of another, and another and, being bold, brave men, began to think aloud about having a railway on which to run the collection. To rebuild the Dorrigo line, with its washouts and overgrowth of lantana, seemed ambitious to the point of unreality. But no-one told them it couldn't be done and they began to do it. During 1986, they ran their first train on the new-old Dorrigo line.

At the same time as rebuilding the track, the group went on gathering its exhibits. As the railways took more and more of the old goods and passenger vehicles out of service, the museum was waiting to buy the best available. They've spent $400 000 so far on a collection which covers most types of locomotives and rolling stock used on the New South Wales Railways, and a restoration program extends into the twenty-first century. Long before that, the hope is to have tourist trains running regularly on the steam line to Dorrigo and, as steam passes further into our history, the Rag-Tag Railway opening a window on the past.

And all because of eccentrics: the steam fanciers of Dorrigo, some of them old railwaymen drawn back to the magic of steam, others young men enthralled by noble old machinery, will tell you that an eccentric is a very necessary part of a steam engine. It's part of the valve gear, whose role is to control the admission of

ECCENTRICS ▲

▲ A BIG COUNTRY

First train to Dorrigo, 27 September 1924.

steam and therefore the speed and power and direction of the engine. That's another definition, one that's not in the *Pocket Oxford*. How nice to think that without the dedication, the effort, the sheer hard work of one kind of eccentric, the other kind, the mechanical kind, the steam-driven kind, might have vanished forever from the language and from the experience of a generation yet to come.

There Were No Foxes in Australia

It was an oversight of Nature, the failure to provide foxes in Australia. Some would have to be obtained, if the Gentry were to have their sport. In Tasmania, of course, they could run down an escaping convict every so often, and in Queensland they sometimes hunted blacks, but in the more genteel colonies like Victoria and South Australia there was a pressing need for furry things to provide for the sporting life. So the same idiocy that brought the rabbit to Australia also brought the fox. For sport.

The Hunt, as it's called, has survived, an anachronism if ever there was one, with rules of dress, ceremonial and etiquette observed as rigidly in twentieth century Australia as in eighteenth century England, an irresistible lure to some, a total joke to others. But always with enough enthusiasts to keep the membership lists full, and sometimes a waiting list in places where the hobby farms proliferate and there's more money round than can be made on the land, and more time for sport than working the land allows. For hunting—Riding To Hounds, it should be called—satisfies several of the urges of man: to dress in a way different from others; to ride horses in ways that have the edge of danger; to observe a system of rules; to take part in rituals; to arouse a socially permissible lust.

Wide open country is the huntsman's friend, closer settlement and the subdivision of land the enemy. Wire fences, especially with a row or two of barb on top, are particularly hated, and a huntsperson with horse, wrapped in several metres of such fence, is a sorry sight indeed. So where possible, and where friendly land-

THE FOX, LIKE THE RABBIT, AN ASSISTED IMMIGRANT FOR THE SAKE OF 'SPORT'.

▲ *A BIG COUNTRY*

ECCENTRICS

owners allow it, the hunt clubs modify the occasional fence, installing safe, and visible, jumping points. A good horse, they say, will jump anything, but better not to take the risk.

No hunter since Diana herself has been able to solve the big problem of hunting, the unpredictable path of the fox. And that's all part of the thrill of the chase, that very unpredictability. Over centuries of the 'pursuit of the uneatable by the unspeakable' the chase has become as ritualised as the strange dress and strange drinks. Where the fox runs the hounds follow, the Master follows the hounds, and the Hunt follows the Master. Simple really, so why do they bother?

It seems it's all inherited. Good hounds beget good hounds. Good horses beget good horses. And, socially, at the Hunt Club affairs, the scent is often picked up which leads to the next generation of huntspersons. All due to those homesick toffs 150 years ago who offered assisted passages to a few British foxes.

OPPOSITE PAGE: *The English hunt, said Oscar Wilde, is 'the unspeakable in full pursuit of the uneatable'. On the edge of Australia's biggest city, Sydney, hunt clubs gather to observe the traditions.*
AUSTRALIAN PICTURE LIBRARY

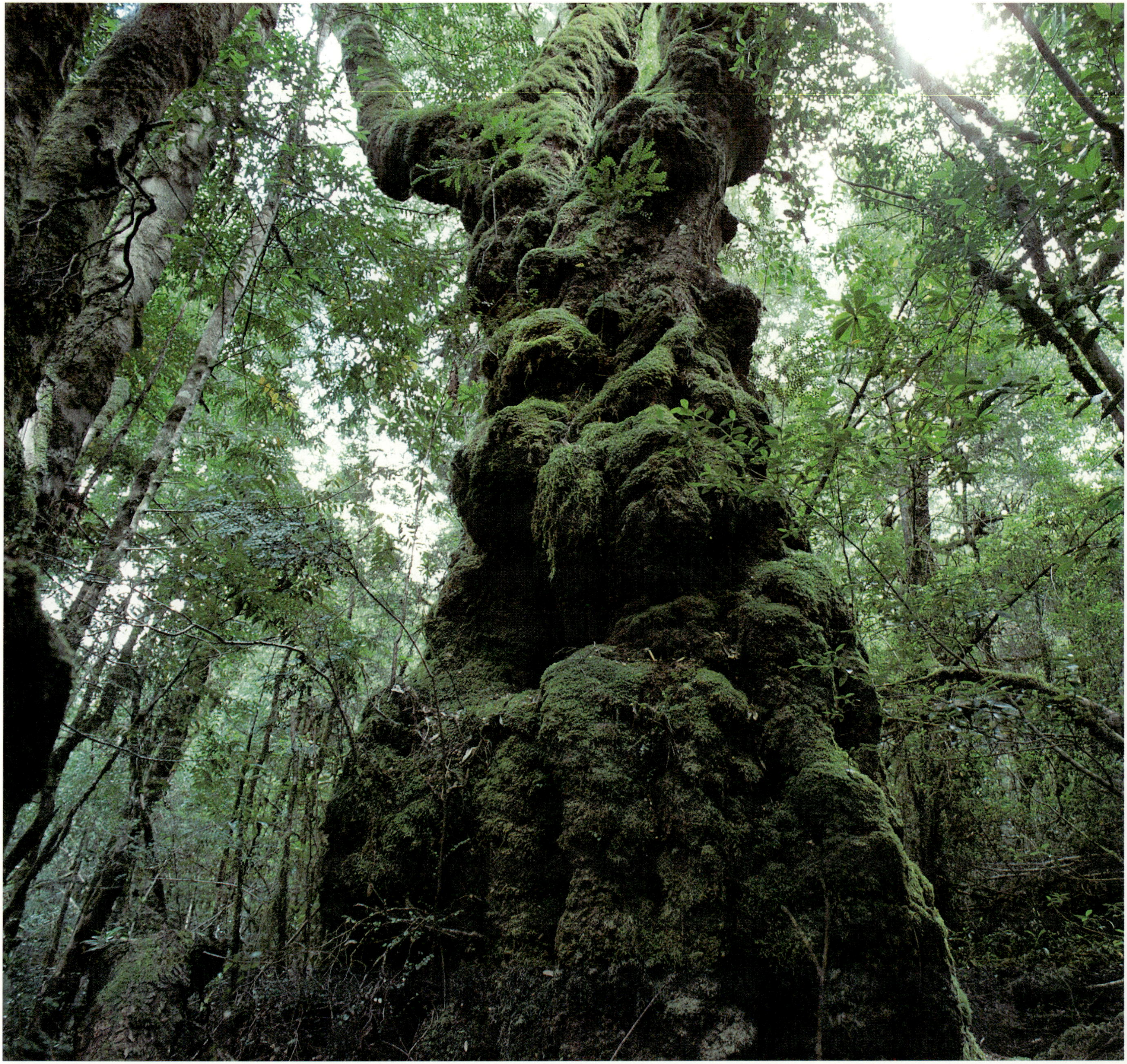

SURVIVORS

A BIG COUNTRY: itself something of a survivor for rare indeed in the television industry is a program whose run lasts so long. Many of its stories have been built around other survivors—people, animals, occupations, lifestyles—and often it has found them just in time, about to yield to changing economics, new tastes, and that strange catch-all called Progress.

It was a form of progress that brought to Australia one of the great survivors, the rabbit. The British settlers thought it was progressive to have some British animals to scamper about under their newly planted British trees. Much later, another form of progress, farming, found the rabbit a menace and decreed it had to go. That was easier said than done and the rabbit survived and survives still, though by an odd quirk of fate Australia now imports rabbit skins for the manufacture of felt hats. That's progress.

Progress brought rapid road transport which threatened to condemn the Australian drover to history. But drought doesn't answer to the demands of progress, and the continuing need to find drought feed for stock means the drover has survived, though his numbers are depleted. As were those of our oldest survivor, the salt-water crocodile, until protection from shooting so increased its numbers that this great prehistoric lizard now eats more people than the much-feared shark.

Progress gets in the way of modern-day Robinson Crusoes, and holiday resorts reach out to untouched islands where once a hermit could survive and enjoy a voluntary exile. And travelling showmen, whose lives are also exiles of a kind, find the appeal of their tented wonders eclipsed by tape-recorded fantasy beamed in to the bush by satellite.

OPPOSITE PAGE: SURVIVOR FROM A VERY OLD FAMILY, AN ANTARCTIC BEECH TREE IN SOUTH-WEST TASMANIA.
KATHIE ATKINSON

The Last Tent Show

The Last Tent Show survived longer than most of its kind. The travelling boxing troupes, a part of bush Australia for a hundred years and more, wore out their welcome everywhere but Queensland by the 1980s. In the other States, the rule-makers had decided we could do without the spectacle they offered. The show inside the shabby tents wasn't always worth the money, but the warm-up, the come-on out the front was pure entertainment. Larry Dulhunty was one of its stars, an ageing star, and the last of his breed.

Larry used to work the national show circuit, taking his tent and his boxers south to north-east to west and back again with his raucous challenge to the local heroes to step in and fight the visiting champ. Often they wanted to fight Larry himself: they'd broken his nose six times, and seven times he'd broken his knuckles on them. Larry Dulhunty had lived hard.

A Big Country found the Dulhunty show in western Queensland, where Larry was still welcome and his challenges would still be met. At fifty-seven, he was getting perilously close to forty years in the business of boxing, having begun as a kid of ten staging fights outside pubs with his mate and collecting coins thrown by watching drunks.

He left home at eleven to become a drover and wound up buckjump riding in the touring Tex Morton Show. A natural knockabout fighter, the Government taught him to be a professional: he was a World War II commando and fought the Kokoda Trail Show at nineteen. There was some money and a lot of kudos in the post-

LARRY DULHUNTY

▲ A BIG COUNTRY

OPPOSITE PAGE:
The Dulhunty tent show at Dajarra, Queensland: 'It's not Madison Square Garden.'

war years in being known as a good knuckle man, and Larry was said to be the best in north-west Queensland. But to make a business of it, Larry latched on to a legend: Jimmy Sharman, the greatest tent man of them all.

Sharman liked Larry and passed on to him the wit and wisdom of life on the board-walk outside the tent, the bass drum booming hypnotically, the ragged row of fighters in tattered dressing gowns posturing threateningly or looking either spaced out or bored. From Jimmy The Great, Dulhunty learned to spruik, to hustle, to manipulate crowds, above all to get the maximum number of people inside his tent and paying for the show they'd already had outside. It was an apprenticeship in showmanship few people have ever had, and it set Larry Dulhunty off on a thirty-year odyssey to every small town from the Kimberleys to Cooktown. *A Big Country* filmed him at Dajarra, Queensland, cleaning up the cow dung before putting up his tent. The place wasn't Madison Square Garden, he observed, and there was a fence post he'd have to clear out of the way in case a fighter hit his head on it and went for the Permanent Knock-Out.

He had a lot to think about because he was presenting more than just a boxing troupe. There was a bit of a show, too, with a singer, a juggler and a guitar player. But the boxing was the big attraction in the north-west, where men were men and liked to rough each other up regularly to prove it. The chance to mix it with visiting professionals was too good to miss, especially if some incidents could be created in advance, carefully contrived by the showman himself. 'We hustle them, yes,' he says cheerfully. 'You could call us the glove hustlers I suppose. We don't hustle with billiard cues or decks of cards or prostitutes. We hustle with the boxing gloves.'

The trips between hustles were getting longer. Changing tastes and compe-

SURVIVORS ▲

▲ *A BIG COUNTRY*

tition from spreading television drove the Dulhunty Show into the real backblocks, driving three thousand kilometres some weeks in search of receding dollars. And that was before videos and satellite television. It was 1980, the next town was Normanton, where fighting was the entertainment. The best fighters in Queensland are there, Larry said, it was their sport. And, sure enough, it was Larry himself they wanted to fight, all fifty-seven years of him. So he'd be in his makeshift ring tonight. Win or lose he'd hope to make money. Strike the tent tomorrow, two or three days on the road and another show, another fight in another town. That was life for Larry Dulhunty: three rounds for fifty dollars; can the local lad last the distance, meet the challenge of this Last of the Glove Hustlers?

OPPOSITE PAGE: *Larry Dulhunty, 40 years a fighter.*

Only for the Rabbits, We'd Be Buggered

ABOVE: *The Trapper: in hard times a way of life.*

OPPOSITE PAGE: *Rabbit shooters. There's still money in the bunny, but the meat is no longer the battler's chicken. Nowadays chicken is cheaper.*
GRENVILLE TURNER/WILDLIGHT

In a vote to select the Great Australian Survivor, the much-cursed rabbit would come out near the top. Of all the immigrants to reach Australian shores, the rabbit has adapted faster and better than most. It copes with flood and fire and, by a system of controlled breeding, it copes with drought and famine. What could man learn from the rabbit?

The rabbit took assisted passage to Australia from England. History says the villain of the piece was one Thomas Austin, who had a property near Geelong, Victoria, and it didn't seem quite like home without some little grey furry animals to scuttle about and be shot for the amusement of the squire and his guests. Tom Austin jumped several rungs of the social ladder in one leap in 1865, when visiting Royalty accepted his invitation to shoot rabbits at Geelong. (The rabbits may later have had their revenge: the visiting Royal found himself the target of a demented gunman in Sydney, who missed.)

Austin's rabbits found Geelong very much to their liking. There were even imported gamekeepers to look after them, the only problem was Austin and his gun-toting guests. Rabbits rarely shift house: hunger and fear are about the only motives that will move them, and they began to spread away from the places with guns. Within ten years, they'd reached the Darling River and tracked along it through northern New South Wales and into southern Queensland. One day, a rabbit or several discovered the Promised Land. Men would later give it a bold but borrowed name, Texas.

SURVIVORS ▲

▲ A BIG COUNTRY

As in hard times, drought times, the rabbit will curtail its breeding through an in-built, environmentally actuated fertility control system, so in times of plenty, rabbits will breed...like rabbits. The Texas district of southern Queensland offered everything a rabbit could want, and its numbers grew beyond count.

Damage grew, too, with rising numbers and the voices of the landowners were raised in anger and despair. But not everyone was angry. Not everyone saw ruin. Some people, who owned no land, ran no sheep, grew no crops, had no jobs, realised that the rabbit could be the poor man's friend: it offered meat, free for the trapping, and highly saleable skins to be tanned, dyed, renamed in French and worn by another species which has only localised fur of its own. The Texas rabbit industry was on its way.

'There was a lot of money about when the rabbits were thick,' the veteran trapper Cliff Beard told *A Big Country*. 'Everyone had plenty of money, and they spent it pretty quick because they knew they could earn it again the next week. Anything up to fifty quid, some of 'em made a hundred quid a week.'

Not all of them spent the big money. Rabbits made possible life on the land for some of the battlers. Skins and carcass sales were the foundation for future farming prosperity. For others, though, the easy money at the peak of the trade drew kids prematurely out of school and round the traps. 'Forty quid for a night's work,' one Texan summed up the lure of rabbiting.

'We had more to do with rabbits than we ever had with school. We never had that much education, never went to school much. Catch rabbits and bush working and ring barking and shearing's all we ever did. I put it this way myself: only for the rabbits, we'd be buggered.'

And many times, it appeared, so were the rabbits. Certainly, men tried

SURVIVORS ▲

hard enough to eradicate them, from Texas as from a thousand other infested districts. The trappers made no difference at all to numbers. For every one they caught above ground, down in the warrens scores more were being conceived in a continuous breeding frenzy. A pair of rabbits, the naturalist-statisticians said, could become five hundred in a single year, a new generation every eight to ten weeks.

In the 1940s, the rabbit supplemented the meat-rationed diet of many Australians. The fur was worth a pound a pound—it made the felt for the diggers' hats, the legends said, but at the end of the war, rural Australia again realised there wasn't going to be room for both farming and the rabbit. The war had produced the virulent poison 1080, for killing mice and rats in grain stockpiles, and it quickly replaced strychnine, arsenic and phosphorus in the chemical war on the warrens.

Science had more to offer: a kind of germ warfare, the disease myxomatosis, was developed in Australian laboratories, a fever, mosquito borne, and attacking only the rabbit. Like a line from the adventures of Brer Rabbit himself, 'This time, Brer Rabbit, this time', science and agriculture confidently expected.

It would rid Australia of rabbits, though a lot of people didn't like it much; it was somehow barbaric the way blinded and agonised animals staggered about for the several days it took them to die. Too many Australians had known in childhood the bunny rabbit toy, the rabbit motif on baby's own first plate and on the nursery wallpaper, the rabbit hero of so many of the first stories read to them.

Myxo, nevertheless, was the toast of the bush, until the remarkable physiology of the rabbit began to fight back. Not every infected rabbit developed the disease. There was an occasional immunity, and immune rabbit mated with im-

TOP: *Star of nursery story, picture book and wallpaper, the rabbit has had a better press than farmers would give him.*
KATHIE ATKINSON

BOTTOM: *The rabbiter: there are easier ways to make a living.*
GRENVILLE TURNER/WILDLIGHT

mune rabbit to produce immune generations. Science changed the mixture of the disease. The rabbit switched his immunity just enough to survive.

No-one in the bush is making much of a living from rabbits any more. They can still be bought in specialist butchers but buyers tend to want to see a pedigree to guarantee that traces of some man-made disease do not linger to flavour the stew. Occasionally when times are bad in the bush, people suggest we might try farming the rabbit. But the rabbit's entrenched enemies react to such ideas with surprising fervour, and authority is wheeled out to say why it can't be done. Yet, in South Australia thirty years ago, an agricultural expert, A Department Man, did a study of rabbit economics in the conditions of the time and found they significantly outperformed sheep as money-makers. He broadcast his findings on the ABC's *Country Breakfast Session*, fortunately under an alias, on the morning of an April the First. There was a witch-hunt, his identity was never proved, he kept his job. But his figures were never successfully challenged. It seemed the man was right.

Back to Texas, and the old trapper Cliff Beard. He respected the rabbits: 'Yeah, they're smart. They've survived all these years we've gone after 'em, so they must be.'

The Drover

'Once we get over those mountains we're gunna strike that real lush feed down there. It's gunna be beautiful going, the tough going will be over then...' (The drover's creed, from Jack Torney).

Not a lot different, really, the drover's optimism from the city man's 'tomorrow's got to be better, it couldn't be any worse'. Or the tired old tale about the grass on the other side of the fence. If A B Paterson was right, and the drover's life has pleasures that the townsfolk never know, it also has more than its share of problems. *A Big Country* found Jack Torney, a drover, grazing his mob in the Long Paddock, the drovers' name for the roads, where in drought times sheep are sent to graze on whatever dusty growth the roadsides offer.

Jack had 5000 sheep in his care, worth at the time $150 000, but worth nothing unless they could be kept alive. That was Jack Torney's problem, and his job: keeping them alive and moving on a journey that would end where it had begun, on the owner's property. But that was a season away, and first there would have to be rain and regrowth. There had been neither since Jack drove the mob off the run, a year ago in time and 1500 kilometres in distance.

The drover, his son Michael, two offsiders and seventeen dogs had kept the mob moving over outback tracks and stock routes, because the law demands movement by travelling stock and in some places sets a minimum of ten kilometres a day. Jack Torney had sometimes covered twice that, because feed and water, not words, were the regulations that governed this drover's life.

JACK TORNEY, DROVER.

▲ A BIG COUNTRY

BELOW AND OPPOSITE PAGE: *A PERIL OF THE LONG PADDOCK—THE ONCE-A-WEEK MIXED TRAIN TO BUSH AUSTRALIA BREAKS INTO THE DROVER'S LINESIDE SEARCH FOR FEED.*

For most of his life Jack had answered to the rules of feed and water. He was a Riverina kid, and his education both ended and began when, at age thirteen, he left school at Balranald to go droving. He'd wanted to do that as long as he could remember. How long? Hard to say. Time didn't mean much to Jack Torney. 'Time means nothing. I'm just looking for feed and water and time doesn't mean a thing. I just keep walkin'.'

He's walking the 5000 sheep towards distant moutains, the Great Divide, which he plans to cross by a track he knows which other drovers won't use because it's through inhospitable country with little to offer man or sheep. But on the other side, his optimism tells him, there it's different. There's got to be better feed on the other side of those mountains. So says the drover's creed. Tricky, though, to get there. The Australia Jack knows has a very different view of travelling stock from the days when the drover was the aristocrat of bush workers and his paths were a clearly reserved network of stock routes now mostly gone. Many of his former tracks and trails are under bitumen, with white lines to guide the fast fools in motor cars who'll tear along the dotted line whether there are sheep there or not. Jack lost his best dog that way, and it still hurts. But to get where he's going, he must venture onto main roads, even onto railways if he has to. There is often good feed alongside the line, if the poisoning or burning gangs haven't been along for a while.

And it would be, wouldn't it, just when 5000 sheep are draped like a dusty blanket across a hundred metres of line, that the once-a-week goods train comes round the bend behind a pair of snarling diesels, air horns trumpeting a challenge to the invaders of its territory. Then follows a scene which is the essence of *A Big Country*, a slice of the kind of life we're still lucky enough to have, and a

SURVIVORS ▲

▲ *A BIG COUNTRY*

conversation that would not have the same flavour anywhere else in the world. The two blue diesels hiss and grind their way to a halt, and over the idling rumble of engines Driver calls to Drover, 'G'day mate. How're you doin?'

Drover: 'G'day. How are yer?'

Driver: 'Get those sheep off the track for us?'

Drover: 'I'll move 'em for you. Yeah, push 'em through easy. Been a good feed on the rail here, we thought we'd eat it out, save you the fires, eh?'

Driver: 'Yeah, no worries.'

Drover: 'Just go through easy, it'll be pretty good.'

Engines grumble back to work, the train eases forward. With a drover left and right, and Ralph the Wonder Dog in the middle, the mob parts like a mud-brown sea and the train passes through.

Life for Jack would be harder if it weren't for Ralph. He's been around since a pup, and top dog since his predecessor second guessed the speed of an approaching car. Now, Jack says, he's worth $5000, though he's not for sale for that, or any other, price. The only thing worth more than a good dog is a good offsider, and Jack's got that too: his son Michael, a natural drover, and nearly ready to set up in business for himself.

'It'd be good to see him go out,' Jack says, 'because the day's coming when there's no young blokes want to go out droving at all.'

But is there any point in training more drovers? Isn't it something of the past, and there's not much need for it now?

'I think it'll keep going for ever in Australia, droving,' Jack says. 'And I hope it does. Because it's part of Australia.'

And he's right. While ever bush Australia turns on its tricks of drought,

OPPOSITE PAGE: *HALOED IN THE GOLD OF SUNSET, SHEEP REMIND THE DROVER OF THEIR VALUE. HE'S KEPT THEM ALIVE AND HEALTHY FOR ANOTHER DAY ON THE ROAD, AND NOW HE WORRIES FOR TOMORROW'S FEED AND WATER.*

▲ A BIG COUNTRY

fire, pasture grubs and other disasters, there will be the need to move sheep to somewhere else and keep them alive until the home paddocks come good again. Even the smartest supercharged diesel road transport is no good at that. And even less use at what Jack Torney and his brothers on the stock routes do best: just keep 'em moving, and find 'em feed and water. The drover's job is safe, while ever the grass grows in the Long Paddock.

Who Was Here First, Anyway?

A creature very like the crocodile inhabited the earth 160 million years ago, occupying a great swathe of the planet from the Nile River in Egypt to northern Australia.

Since the far more recent coming of humans, the two species have coexisted in something less than harmony. Humans have either hunted the crocodile or worshipped it, feared it and drawn it on the walls of their caves, worn its skin in triumph on their feet or carried it in elegant fashion, shaped and sewn as a handbag. And, finally, in late twentieth century Australia, they have enacted laws to protect it. In all the millennia, the crocodile's attitude to humans hasn't changed one iota: they remain good to eat. And in northern Australia protection laws are having their effects and crocodile numbers are increasing at the same time as the Australian wilderness has become an international tourist destination.

There is a simple sum here. More people plus more crocodiles equals more meetings between crocodiles and people. Such meetings, if unrehearsed and unexpected, have an almost inevitable result: the crocodile gets its dinner. The visitor, if he or she were alive to realise it, would get the point of that catchy little song they used to sing about the crocodile. 'Don't be taken in by the friendly grin, he's just imagining how well you'd fit within his skin.'

Perversely, a crocodile attack in the wilds of northern Australia will not repel the tourists. Rather, it will draw them. And if the victim is a glamorous young American woman, it will make world news and would-be adventuring holidaymakers will add a

Waiting for lunch, Northern Territory.
KATHIE ATKINSON

▲ A BIG COUNTRY

BELOW: *Warning sign, Northern Territory—but who would want to swim here anyway.*
BARRY SKIPSEY/NORTHERN TERRITORY TOURIST COMMISSION

OPPOSITE PAGE: *Teeth that can hold a horse, and jaws strong enough to stamp out panels in a car factory... The sleepy image is deceptive. When lunch comes close, the saltwater crocodile can move with the speed of a striking snake.*
KATHIE ATKINSON

new destination to their air tickets, carve a new notch on the camera bag.

Given its long-term tenancy of northern Australia, the crocodile had a peaceful existence until very recent times. An unwary Aborigine would sometimes vary the creatures' diet, the discovery of gold and the epic treks of oriental miners across the north from Darwin to the goldfields were other variations, then settlers provided cattle which drank at their peril from some northern rivers. Crocodile attacks on cattle or horses, or an occasional close shave for an overconfident stockman, would bring out the shooting parties. A crocodile or several would be shot and the immediate problem considered solved.

That changed with the post-war prosperity of Europe. There was plenty of money to spend on dressing up, and fashion, casting around for something new to be declared fashionable, found crocodile skin. The shoemakers and leather workers wanted only the belly skin, the rest was unworkable. The skins came to be worth very big money indeed, and with old Lee Enfield .303s bought cheaply from army disposals, the professionals and people who fancied themselves to be professionals moved in. Anything over thirty centimetres long was fair game. The big ones were shot for their belly skins, the carcasses left to rot where they lay, and the young ones too small to skin, were killed, stuffed and mounted in fierce poses and sold at outlandish prices to gullible tourists who ventured north on the old passenger boats like the *Manunda*, *Manoora* and *Kanimbla*.

The hunters shot out Arnhem Land in the 1940s, the Kimberleys and the Gulf in the 'fifties and Cape York in the 'sixties. Protection came too late and by the time Queensland, last State to protect the crocodile, acted, the last of our prehistoric creatures had been shot to near extinction. But as befits a survivor of 160 million years, the crocodile population recovered. A grown crocodile, one of

100

SURVIVORS ▲

▲ A BIG COUNTRY

OPPOSITE PAGE, LEFT: *IN THE CAUSE OF SCIENCE, A RESEARCHER TAKES A RISKY CENSUS OF NEXT YEAR'S LIKELY CROCODILE POPULATION.* RIGHT: *Do this in a film with a stuffed crocodile and fame and fortune will result. But the slightest misjudgment in this tagging project and the winner is the one with the teeth.*

the most fearsome creatures in all nature, has few things to fear in the wild. But nature, to preserve a balance and to protect the world from being up to the neck in crocodiles, makes the young crocodile highly vulnerable. At the egg stage, every animal and bird around finds the crocodile product appetising, and the eggs, as well as the hatchlings, are often eaten by other crocodiles.

Armour-plated, fearfully armed with teeth that can hold a horse and jaws strong enough to stamp out panels in a car factory, capable of amazing speed of movement on land or water, the crocodile nevertheless is acutely affected by its environment, particularly by the temperature. It is a cold-blooded beast, and must spend much of its time regulating its body temperature to around 30°C. That is why it lies in the sun on a mud bank, warming up, and sliding occasionally and with deceptive sloth, into the water to cool off again. Too hot or too cold and it will lose its appetite and its desire to breed. Its normally acute senses will be dulled and it might even die. One startling discovery has been how important a role temperature has on its life. The temperature of the eggs during incubation decides the sex of the young crocodile. It has no chromosomes.

By one of the giant steps science occasionally makes, a discovery has been made about the crocodile embryo that can be applied to the forming human baby. Mark Ferguson, a professor of medicine at Britain's Manchester University, joined a crocodile research program in the Northern Territory. His specialty is human birth defects, such as cleft lip and palate. It has been found that crocodiles have a roof of the mouth just like that of humans, and because a crocodile develops, like a chicken, in an external egg, experiments with a valuable human application can be done as the embryo grows. There are people in the Northern Territory, wildlife rangers, brave enough to rob crocodile nests of some of their

SURVIVORS

eggs in the interests of science and ultimately of the crocodile population. Only a tiny percentage of the fifty or more eggs each female lays will hatch out, predators will get the rest. So the wildlife people can build up numbers quickly by collecting eggs and hatching them artificially. This technique may lead eventually to crocodile farming, the breeding of the creatures either to restock areas where natural populations are gone or to produce skins, made even more valuable by an international ban on trading the skins of animals killed in the wild.

Dr Grahame Webb headed the Territory research project which could, he said, make productive big areas of swampland that are now liabilities to the cattle stations of which they are part. Fenced off, and stocked with crocodiles, the liabilities could be made assets. What Dr Webb proposed was the permanent integration of the crocodile into the life and economy of regions of northern Australia. Properly managed, he believed, such a project would protect not only one of the great survivors of this planet, but also the delicate wetlands environment in which the crocodile thrives.

Tourism is the Northern Territory's most promising industry. Crocodiles are high in the tourists' expectations of a frontier holiday. Getting the two together in such a way that neither damages the other is a problem for both tour managers and wildlife specialists. Crocodile attacks have occurred at places where signposts clearly state the dangers and are widely ignored. Freddy Hunter, one of the old-time shooters, recalls that he and his mates never had any trouble with crocodiles. They knew how dangerous the creatures were, and treated them with due respect. But nowadays, he says, people ignore the danger and swim anywhere at all. And to a crocodile, nothing's changed: when dinner swims by in a bikini, you grab it.

No Place for a Hermit

Earlier in this twentieth century there were still to be found islands of isolation, places without people, to which a romantic or a soul disappointed in life or love, or frequently both, could escape to live as he or she chose. Nowadays, we call it dropping out. But to call someone a drop-out is condemnatory. There is an older, nicer word: hermit. That is the word to describe the solitary painter of Bedarra Island.

Noel Wood. In Melbourne of the 1930s the name appeared discreetly on portraits of the socially prominent and the financially well-to-do. Skill as a portrait artist kept Noel Wood a step ahead of the deprivations of the Depression, but did little for his professional satisfaction. A successful exhibition brought him 250 of that most pretentious unit of medical, legal and artistic currency, the guinea. (A guinea was one pound and one shilling, twenty-one shillings or $2.10. It was nothing more than a backdoor way of adding a sneaky five per cent to the price of an article or a service. Long featured on the bills of such professionals as doctors and lawyers, and on the price tickets of paintings, race-horses, antiques and *objets d'art*, by the time of its well-deserved demise at the coming of decimal currency the guinea was being used surreptitiously to raise the price of refrigerators and washing machines.)

In the depressed Australia of the 1930s, 250 of these guinea things represented a small fortune for a young artist barely into his twenties. Certainly it promised liberation from painting portraits of pampered women. More, carefully managed it was enough to

NOEL WOOD

▲ A BIG COUNTRY

OPPOSITE PAGE, LEFT: *A SPLENDID ISOLATION—NOEL WOOD AND HIS ISLAND DOMAIN.* **RIGHT:** *POLITE, BUT TO THE POINT, THE TIMELESS PLEA OF THE HERMIT.*

finance his dream: to live in solitude somewhere remote, an island preferably, and to enjoy there sun and sea and a lifetime of painting things more beautiful than the faces of the wives, daughters and mistresses of establishment Melbourne.

Noel Wood bought an old car, a Model T Ford, and in 1936 drove north out of Melbourne forever. He chased the sun to its year-round lair in the tropics, and when he reached the line of Capricorn at Rockhampton, Queensland, he began his real search, along 1500 kilometres of coast nature had liberally littered with islands which the Queensland Government was quite happy to sell in whole or in part. The search ended north of Townsville, where he found an island called Bedarra. He bought a headland and two beaches, and the Hermit of Bedarra was at home.

But his elaborate planning was flawed. He overlooked the practicalities—not the first artistic dreamer to do so—that without food and shelter, even the artist can't survive, and when he has chosen a life in which he must grow his own food and build his own shelter, the business of simply surviving cuts heavily into the time that was going to be devoted utterly to art.

Over a period, however, art became less important than the enjoyment of life. Noel Wood became a tropical islander and taught himself the living skills of an islander. He learned to grow taro, staple food of islanders for millennia, and he learned the generosity of the tree of life, the coconut palm, which offers an islander food, drink and the materials for shelter.

In building, gardening, fishing and sometimes painting, Noel Wood spent two-thirds of a lifetime, half a century of non-involvement in some of humanity's greatest achievements and worst disasters. The world went to war; on Bedarra Island, the coconut palms Noel Wood planted grew tall and fruitful. The Cold

SURVIVORS ▲

▲ A BIG COUNTRY

OPPOSITE PAGE: *DOOMED BY ITS OWN BEAUTY, BEDARRA AWAITED INEVITABLE DISCOVERY.*

War began; on Bedarra, it was always warm. Australia boomed in post-war prosperity; there were good seasons for taro on Bedarra. Another war came and went, Korea. Yet another, Vietnam; the tides rose and fell on Wood's two private beaches. The jet aeroplane brought the world to within twenty-four hours of Australia; Noel Wood acquired a small boat. Men walked on the moon, but their footsteps did nothing to dim its light which shone silver on the palms and waters of Bedarra.

Noel Wood kept his back firmly turned on the world and trusted the world would maintain its disinterest in him. But it was a one-sided arrangement. In business offices far away, the sons of the kind of people he'd escaped from half a century before were making plans for his world, and he was about to learn he should have bought the whole island.

One day noxious yellow machines came lumbering ashore off their barges, and Noel Wood found himself a potential neighbour of the tourist boom. Time and commerce had caught up with Bedarra and its inhabitant. There was money to be made from forgotten islands. Glossy brochures were being printed and distributed in newly affluent tourist markets far away, where a new generation of dreamers planned to drop out for a week, to be castaway for twelve nights and thirteen days including air-fares-and-transfers-twin-share-accommodation.

One by one, the islands of the Queensland coast had fallen to the new invaders, had featured in saturation advertising and appeared on vulgar and suggestive T-shirts. Now it was the turn of Bedarra. They were about to make it No Place for a Hermit.

It's not hard to make life difficult for a solitary man. You simply raise his taxes, make his land so expensive he can't afford it any more, and so he moves.

SURVIVORS ▲

▲ *A BIG COUNTRY*

It's been done often in heartless and corrupt cities to clear out old residents and facilitate the demolition of their homes so the site can be used for new and monstrous office blocks and shopping malls. It can be done just as easily to a loner on a distant island. Up go the taxes. In come the developers' offers. Out goes the loner, after half a century. In come the tourists.

Perhaps a friendly island resort guide will tell the visitors the story of the Hermit of Bedarra Island. Perhaps he will go down in what passes for folklore on island resorts. They might commission a Noel Wood painting for the reception foyer, showing the island as it was in its primitive times before it gained the benefits of development.

They might even name a bar for him.

OPPOSITE PAGE: *Noel Wood, the Hermit of Bedarra*

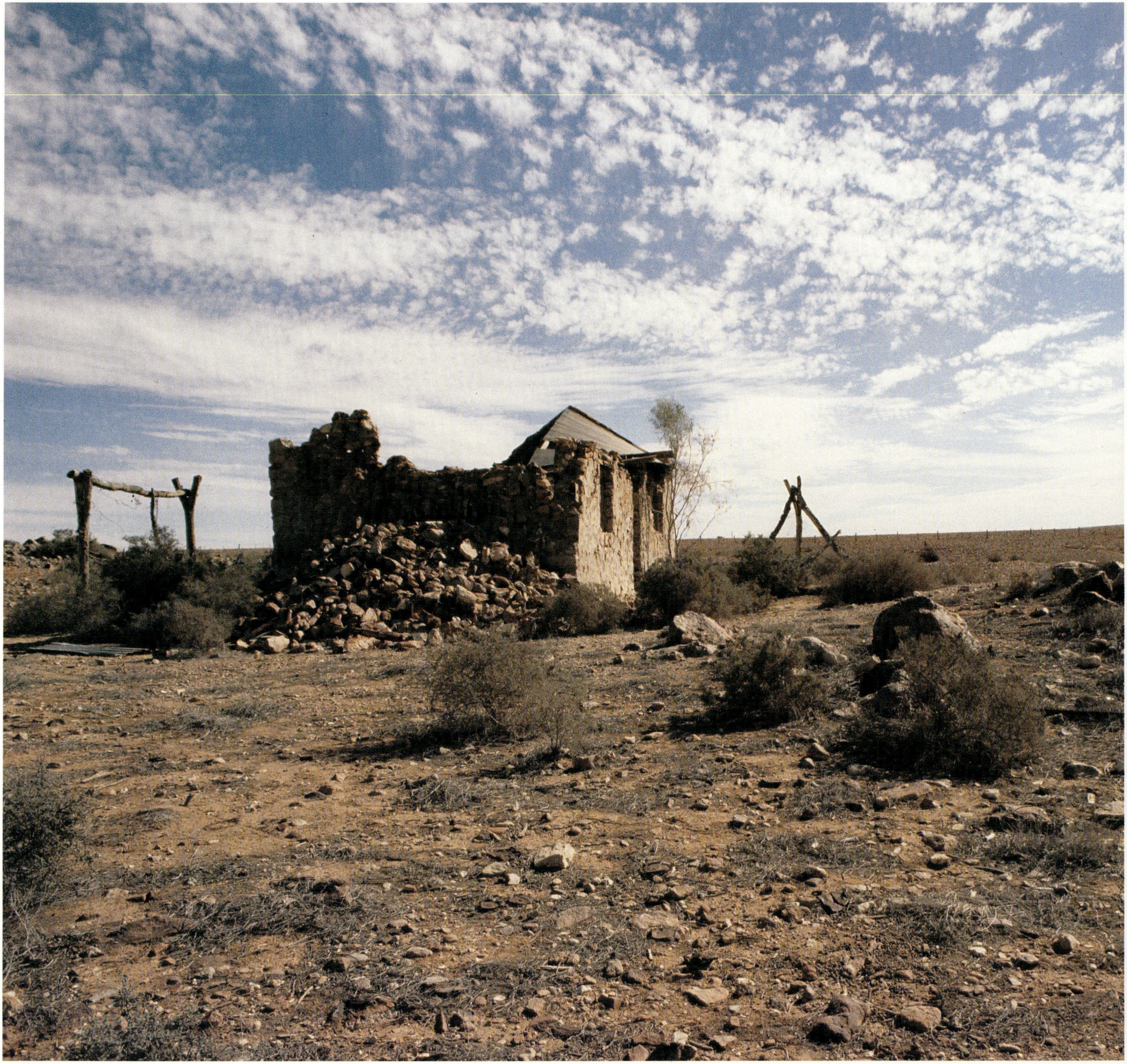

LOSERS

ALL TOO OFTEN these days, the Australian bush is no place for a koala. Once hunted for its fur, now robbed of food and shelter as forestry, land-clearing and urban sprawl destroy its favoured trees, beset by disease and its survival seriously at risk, the koala is a real Australian loser.

There are others, animal and human, for whom this has not been the Lucky Country: Burke and Wills, the explorers, found it unforgiving, even murderous; Amy Pulsford, a shepherd in the high country of Tasmania, found it always hard and lately tragic; the people of a small Victorian town whose main industry is welfare haven't a lot to feel lucky about; and the survivors of one of the blackest chapters in our history, the sugar slave trade, don't yet feel they belong after four generations.

These five widely disparate stories record another side of life in A Big Country.

OPPOSITE PAGE: THE SETTLERS HAVE GONE WITH FAILURE. THE SOIL HAS GONE WITH THE WIND. A PICTURE OF A LAND DESTROYED. KATHIE ATKINSON

Too Much Like a Teddy

'It's flea-ridden, it piddles on you, it stinks and it scratches. It's a rotten little thing.'

In the annals of quotable quotes from Australian politics, this opinion of one of our national symbols, the koala, expressed by a Minister for Sport, Recreation and Tourism, alias the Minister for Selling Australia, has a place of its own.

The problem *with* koalas is the same as the problem *for* koalas: they look too much like teddy bears. So when they fail to do what we expect of them, or do things to—or upon—us that we neither want nor expect, then some of us describe them in terms less than endearing, as did the Minister of the Crown In Charge Of Holidays, Koalas, and Running and Jumping About.

The Honourable the Minister for Sport, Recreation and Tourism—the title itself a comment on our society and the extent to which we've allowed the bureaucracy to inflict itself upon us (next we'll have a Ministry of Fun, and a Minister for Good Times)—was a bit pee-ved with koalas. But the opinion delivered by the offending koala could be interpreted as the considered opinion of the entire species. Because the koala owes us little. It and its fellows have but two problems: the food supply is running out, and a disease is threatening to eradicate the whole species by getting in the way of its reproduction. Both problems are products of European settlement of the koala's homeland. Any wonder that the representative koala delivered itself of a warm, moist opinion on the person of a Minister of the Crown.

STAR OF STAMP AND TELEVISION COMMERCIAL, VICTIM OF NEGLECT AND DEVELOPMENT, A HARD-DONE-BY SYMBOL OF AUSTRALIA.

▲ A BIG COUNTRY

OPPOSITE PAGE: *EVERY TOURIST WANTS TO SEE A KOALA, BUT THEIR PROTECTORS FEAR THAT THEIR FUTURE IS DOUBTFUL.*

Yet it was hardly fair of the animal to blame poor John Brown. The Hon The Min was, after all, merely the representative of 200 years of Browns and Smiths and Joneses whose cumulative effects on the koala population had been disastrous. The Hon John achieved his infamy in the world of the koala simply by the default of others: he was the first Australian Minister of Anything in quite a long while even to mention the animal.

Few creatures of wild Australia have shared the simultaneous celebrity and neglect of the koala. It was lucky to survive early settlement at all because, like everything else that moved in the bush, it was a target for the gun-happies and was a sitting target more literally than most animals. Koala-skin rugs were not unknown in the years before Government declared the animals protected. Protection, though, meant nothing more than legislating that koalas should not be shot at. It did nothing about protecting the animals' habitat and food sources and made no effort to increase our knowledge of this unique creature. To this day, our total real knowledge of the koala is contained in a few scientific papers that together would make barely half a day's reading.

Yet it has been used to decorate items as diverse as postage stamps and tea towels. It has starred in television commercials and been afflicted with a most unbecoming American accent to lure tourists to fly on one particular airline. It has been exported, with generally fatal results, as a goodwill gesture to foreign zoos: goodwill to the zoos, maybe, but certainly not to the travelling koalas. It has been subjected to all the indignities the merchants of hype can devise. In a zoo in Sydney there is even a koala named Ryoichi Sasakawa, in honour of a Japanese philanthropist.

The story of the koala presented by *A Big Country* was a bleak condemna-

LOSERS ▲

▲ A BIG COUNTRY

OPPOSITE PAGE:
TOP AND BOTTOM LEFT: THE KOALA HOSPITAL, PORT MACQUARIE.
BOTTOM RIGHT: JEAN STARR, A VOICE FOR KOALA PROTECTION.

tion of national neglect of an animal which almost anywhere else in the world would be regarded as a national treasure. We know so little about the species that when an animal becomes sick in captivity, or is found sick in the bush, there is almost nothing that can be done to save its life. Nor can the koala help itself: victims of the disease which afflicts a tragic proportion of koalas curl up at the foot of a tree, their heads in their laps, and wait to die. It's not the disease that kills them: they die slowly, of starvation. It is the saddest sight in the Australian bush.

Awareness that something horrible was happening to these appealing animals led to the formation in the early 1970s of the Koala Preservation Society at Port Macquarie, New South Wales. With little professional help, this group of mainly amateur naturalists gathered more knowledge of the koala than anyone had collected before, and they set up a koala hospital to try to find treatments for animals found dying in the bush.

Jean Starr, a founding member of the Society, told *A Big Country* that on top of disease and destruction of habitat, koalas faced another major threat from within their own species: the animals were intensely territorial and young males looking for a personal territory were rebuffed so often by their established elders that they seemed to give up, to yield to a form of stress, to just lie down and die. The more that was learned about koalas, Jean Starr said, the deeper the realisation of how much was still unknown. Food, for example: koalas ate the leaves of only certain species of gum trees, but were even more selective than that and ate only from certain trees. And at certain times of year, they'd stop eating some species altogether. They appeared to need four essential types of leaves, and plenty of them, to maintain nutritional health, but even with the best of food, they were constantly vulnerable to the disease *Chlamydia psittaci*.

LOSERS ▲

▲ A BIG COUNTRY

Chlamydia came to Australia with European settlement, carried perhaps by pets or farm animals. A Brisbane veterinarian, Steven Brown, believes this one disease is responsible for the four conditions which increasingly plague the koala population: pneumonia, blindness, urinary tract infection and sterility. The same organism causes trachoma in humans, which, untreated, leads to blindness. Steven Brown believes that the koala, confronted by the chlamydia organism only since European settlement, is entirely without immunity to it. What's desperately needed, he says, is a treatment for animals already infected and a vaccine for those still healthy.

Equally urgent is the need for protection of the koala's remaining environment. It is being marooned in small pockets of scrub as forestry, land development and urban expansion invade the bush. In the Port Macquarie area, the Koala Preservation Society has planted corridors of koala food trees linking known colonies so that the animals will not be isolated by development. It's a simple and economical tactic, Jean Starr says, and could be used almost anywhere where people are interested in creating an environment they can share with animals as delightful as the koala.

When Australia made its goodwill gifts of koalas to zoos in Japan, the three receiving zoos spent the equivalent of twelve million dollars preparing artificial environments for the animals. Some such dollars, paid as royalties perhaps, or for appearance fees in advertisements, might ensure there will continue to be koalas living free in a natural environment in Australia. The way things are shaping now in the threatened world of the koala, its survival is far from assured.

Whatever would we print on our souvenir tea towels then, or sell to the tourists in the kitsch shops?

Explorers of *A Big Country* always seemed to come in pairs. At least, that was the way the history books used to present them, and if the teacher was careless with pronunciation, the names would run together into some odd combinations: Human Hovell, Bassenflinders, Burkenwills. It took Lenny Lower, the great comic writer, to remind us that the one trio in the annals of our exploration, Blaxland, Lawson and Wentworth, crossed the Blue Mountains and discovered three railway stations.

Learned in an age less questioning of heroes, the story of Australian exploration was filled with noble aims and brave deeds. Much later, one made the discovery that the explorer's trade contained its share of rogues, rascals, self-promoters and men not beyond doctoring a map to show where they wished they'd been. One discovered, too, that Robert O'Hara Burke, tragic co-hero of that epic attempt at a south–north continental crossing, was indeed a bit of a berk.

Or was he? Tom Bergin, a veterinary scientist at Sydney's Taronga Zoo, had a long-term interest in Burke and felt that history re-visited, the newer, more direct, knock-'em-off-their-perches school of history, was less than fair to the dashing Irishman. After all, Bergin rationalised, Burke had failed in effect by only one day to succeed in a bold enterprise: just twenty-four hours was the difference between acknowledgment as a hero of exploration and revilement as an impetuous and foolish amateur, incapable of exploration beyond the route from one Melbourne social event to the next, and

'I am Going to the Gulf'

THE EXPEDITIONERS. FROM BOTTOM LEFT, CLOCKWISE: MCHUGH, NUGGET, BERGIN AND FRANK.
KATHIE ATKINSON

▲ A BIG COUNTRY

BELOW: *A PORTRAIT OF ROBERT O'HARA BURKE CARVED IN A TREE NEAR THE EXPEDITION'S BASE CAMP SITE.*
KATHIE ATKINSON

OPPOSITE PAGE: *THE 'DIG TREE', COOPERS CREEK, SA, A LANDMARK OF EXPLORATION GONE WRONG.*
KATHIE ATKINSON

responsible for the deaths of his colleagues and himself.

There was one test that even a century later could be applied: retrace the Burke and Wills expedition. Do it the way they'd done, the same equipment and the same supplies. Tom Bergin, twentieth century scientist, began his research.

He found that in August, 1860, Burke accepted the commission of the exploration committee of the Victorian Philosophical Institute to form and lead a cross-continental expedition whose objective would be the Gulf of Carpentaria. A base camp would be established at Cooper's Creek, and the expedition proper would set out from there. Tom Bergin decided Cooper's Creek would be his starting point. He took leave from work, gathered together $10 000 and a camel specialist, Paddy McHugh, from Gulgong in New South Wales, and recruited a Northern Territory camel handler, an Aboriginal who liked to be called Nugget, and his young son, Frank.

Burke had opted for comfort in his preparations. He left Melbourne in charge of the biggest expedition the colony had ever seen—twenty-four men, thirty camels, twenty tonnes of stores. Impatient with the slow progress of his unwieldy caravan, Burke divided his party and dashed on ahead to set up the base camp at Cooper's Creek. His haste was later to be harshly criticised and blamed in part for the tragic end to the expedition, but Burke had been told South Australia was sending a rival expedition with the same northern destination and the honour of his Victorian sponsors, as well as of Burke himself, was at stake. They were big on that sort of rivalry in the Melbourne of the 1860s, perhaps it was a precursor of today's ritualistic annual dash to Canberra by State Premiers.

But the competitive edge was false, as such motivators often are. No-one told Burke, perhaps no-one knew, that the South Australians weren't proceeding.

122

LOSERS ▲

▲ A BIG COUNTRY

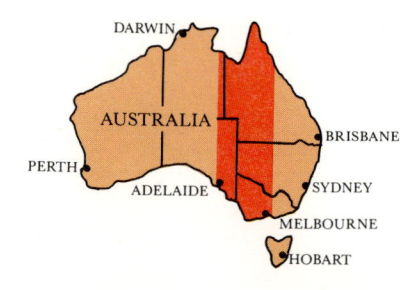

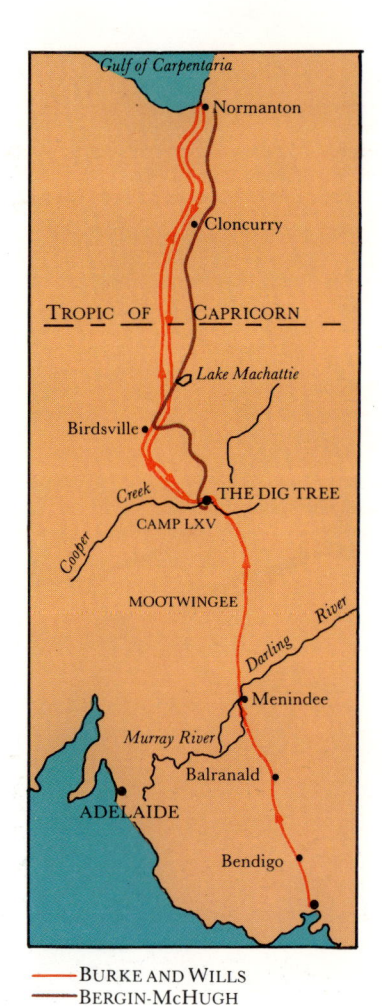

There was no challenge, no race, no need for suicidal haste, but Burke dashed on. At Cooper's Creek, he subdivided his party again and set out for the Gulf.

A big talker, this Robert O'Hara Burke. He said loudly and often in Melbourne that the success of the expedition was more important to him than his life. Or, he added ominously, the lives of his men. What his men thought of that is not recorded.

Ten days before Christmas, 1860, Burke, Wills, Gray and King left Cooper's Creek on the unknown track to the Gulf. The unknown country, the mystery of what might lie beyond the next sandhill, was a factor missing from Bergin and McHugh's re-creation. They knew what lay ahead: nothing. Just endless, empty country. Burke and Wills had the hope of finding perhaps an inland sea, a lost civilisation, gold, fame and medals, 'a totally new country', Tom Bergin said, 'and they would be the men to find it. This was Burke's idea of explorers. They were men who got medals and became famous, and I think that was what he was after. It's just that he picked a bad place to do it, because once you get past the Darling—and the same thing happened to all the explorers out here—the further they push the worse it gets. They were looking for inland seas, cities, God knows what else, and they just weren't there. There was nothing.'

Our reactions to a hostile environment don't change much with progress and sophistication. Bergin knew where he was going and what he'd find there. He knew that if he got into real trouble, help would not be too far away. Hell, he even had film crews criss-crossing his path, because *A Big Country* had chosen his expedition as a major film effort to celebrate the two-hundredth edition of the program. Yet despite all this, the country was getting to him: 'There's a timeless quality out here. It becomes completely irrelevant what time it is. Not only does a

124

LOSERS ▲

day of your life become insignificant, but after a while two or three days become insignificant.

A PLAQUE PERPETUATES THE FAMOUS MESSAGE.
KATHIE ATKINSON

> *I think if you were out here long enough, you'd end up thinking your whole damn lifetime was insignificant. Because, you know, you could live and die out here and absolutely nothing would be changed at all.*
>
> *You start out and you just walk and walk, and you get into a rhythm. You're walking in a coma, you're floating away, completely dissociated from the rest of your body, and I think the landscape helps a bit, too, because it all floats after about eleven, twelve o'clock.*

They had Burke's diaries, and so set the pace of the new expedition at the recorded progress of the original. Tom Bergin, the veterinarian, saw signs of problems the historians had missed: the camels were packing up, they couldn't take the pace. If the camel is rightly called the Ship of the Desert, then he's a tramp steamer, rather than a mail clipper. He'll plod along all day at his own speed, but push him too hard and he breaks down. The camels were breaking down on Bergin and McHugh just as, 117 years before, other camels had failed Burke and Wills.

The people involved were having their problems, too. Nugget, the Aboriginal camel handler and his boy, Frank, had never been personally involved in this white man's madness and, as the going toughened, they withdrew into personal isolation already established by the language barrier. Paddy McHugh was worried about his camels and, undriven by the need to prove or disprove anything, was feeling the monotony.

'Let's face it,' he told Tom Bergin, 'this trip is monotonous, it's a real pain

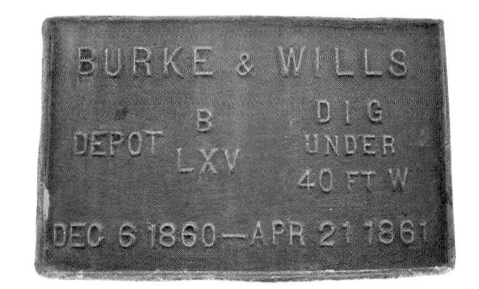

▲ A BIG COUNTRY

OPPOSITE PAGE: TO BURKE AND WILLS, THE UNKNOWN COUNTRY OFFERED THE MYSTERY OF WHAT MIGHT LIE AHEAD.
NOELINE KELLY/AUSTRALIAN PICTURE LIBRARY

in the neck. You get up, you walk twenty-five, thirty miles a day [about forty to fifty kilometres], five or six days a week, then have one day off and get up and do it again.'

Weirdly but understandably, Paddy McHugh was voicing a century-old echo of the words of Robert O'Hara Burke: 'Mr Wills puts us a few days from the Gulf. I will admit there are arguments now in favour of returning: in particular, the state of our animals and food.

'But I will have none of them,' Burke had added. 'I am going to the Gulf.'

Strong in the minds of the less heroic Bergin and McHugh is the realisation that arrival at the Gulf isn't the end of the journey. It is only the halfway point. Perhaps that practicality didn't occur to the driven Burke until too late. Certainly, his diaries have little to say in advance about the return journey. Bergin and McHugh are a week behind schedule, their camels are sore and malnourished, more than half the food is gone. They are in a situation very close to that of Burke and Wills, and Bergin realises that the three months Burke allowed himself for the return trip was impossible. They find Burke's final camp, his blazed ring of fifteen trees mostly still there, and next day, Bergin and McHugh reach a channel of brackish water, fringed by mangroves. It is the water of the Gulf of Carpentaria.

'The camels are buggered,' Paddy McHugh sums up with bushman's finality.

'Camels need two weeks' rest before further work, therefore return trip cancelled,' reads Tom Bergin's telegram sent south by bush radio.

'Why the camels are buggered is because we had too much weight, far too much weight,' Paddy McHugh says. 'We could get back there [Cooper's Creek] no sweat at all, and we could probably go awful close to doing it within the three

LOSERS ▲

months, but we'd lose a couple of camels, there'd be no risk about that.'

That wouldn't have worried the dashing Irishman O'Hara Burke: he had said loudly and very publicly in Melbourne that he would sacrifice his own life and the lives of his men in the cause of success in this singularly unimportant, even lunatic, venture. The lives of a few camels would have been of no account. So Burke turned round and set off back, at the same pace he'd maintained northbound. And so his camels died, and so did he, and so did two of the three—Wills and Gray—who had entrusted their lives to his leadership. Because Burke had no two weeks to 'waste' on the recovery of camels. He had told his base camp at Cooper's Creek he would be back in three months. Those who manned it were to wait three months, then leave, their duty done. They took him at his word: on 21 April 1861, the base camp people at Cooper's Creek buried some food and carved on a gum tree the famous message: 'Dig 3 FT. N.W. APR. 21 1861.' And they left for the south, the Darling River, and Life.

Seven hours later on that tragic day, Burke and Wills reached the Cooper's Creek base camp. Imagine the building excitement as they neared it. Imagine the feeling of breaking camp on the final morning, the day of arrival, the beating of those wretched camels into a last burst of speed through familiar country to the camp site, the shouting through the silent bush, the first doubts when shouts echoed unreturned, the growing disbelief, the panic, the inevitable feeling of betrayal by the empty campsite, and the message, 'Dig', and that awful, awful, date: 21 April 1861.

The mark was still on that tree, Tom Bergin found, certainly one of the most tragic messages in the history of exploration: 'When they dug, they found food and a note...saying that the party had left that morning to go back down to the Darling. They were too weak, and their camels were too weak, for them to follow. So they ate what they could, and then headed down the creek towards Adelaide. The camels died not long down the creek, and both Burke and Wills died. Their graves are just down there.'

Extract from a two-way radio interview with Tom Bergin, giving his camels two weeks' rest at the Burke and Wills camp site on the edge of the Gulf of Carpentaria:

Interviewer: 'Why are you giving it away?'

Bergin: 'The camels are knocked up, and we've got to spell 'em here for a couple of weeks before we can work 'em again. Over.'

Interviewer: 'What does that say about the theory?'

Bergin: 'No good, mate.'

Interviewer: 'Surely there must be more than that. Were you wrong?'

Bergin: 'Yeah, that's right.'

Interviewer: 'What d'you think of Burke and Wills now?'

Bergin: 'I think they were pretty marvellous men.'

Extract from the expedition diary of Robert O'Hara Burke, 21 April 1861: 'We marched 30 miles and reached our depot at Cooper's Creek in the evening, expecting a welcome from the men we had left there. There was nobody, nothing but a message blazed on a tree, and the date April 21st, today.'

The Good Shepherd

For a hundred years sheep have grazed the summer pastures of Tasmania's high country. For a hundred years there's been work there for shepherds, one of the oldest human occupations. One of the shepherds was Amy Pulsford, daughter and grand-daughter of shepherds, a member of a family who'd known no other life, a basic life whose pace and place were dictated by the needs of sheep. Amy had been there since she was six.

When we first came, things were really hard and there wasn't much food, there wasn't much money, and there was a big family of us, a family of eleven. I suppose I followed Dad's footprints, and when I was a little girl I used to wag school, go and hide behind a bush until the school bus had gone, then make out I was in a terrible hurry and Dad would say, 'Well, you've missed the school bus again,' and I'd say, 'Oh beaut, I can go with you now.'

Leaving home as a young adult, Amy went to live in the high country and for ten years lived alone in almost total isolation: three months a year under snow, finding feed for the sheep as best she could and waiting for the thaw to venture out herself to the nearest shops. In this harshest of the environments Australia has to offer, Amy had two children and cared for them through early childhood. No electricity, of course; no telephone, no available help, no security if anything went wrong. But it was not the isolation that forced her out, it was the need for schooling for the children. She left the high country for a village with a school.

AMY PULSFORD

OPPOSITE PAGE: *AMY PULSFORD, SHEPHERD. THE HORSE, THE DOG AND THE RIFLE ARE MODERN TOUCHES TO A CALLING THOUSANDS OF YEARS OLD.*

LOSERS ▲

▲ A BIG COUNTRY

OPPOSITE PAGE: *THERE WERE FEW STRAIGHT LINES IN THE LIFE OF A TASMANIAN SHEPHERD—THE PRESSURE OF NATURE SET THE SHAPE OF LIFE.*

The relative civilisation she returned to was rapidly changing. Tasmania is the Australian centre of hydro-electricity and it has a Hydro-Electric authority so good at what it does, and so enthusiastic about it, that it keeps on building dams and hydro stations whether it needs them or not, much in the fashion of the Canadian beaver for whom dam building is a way of life. Tasmania, after the Hydro, is very different from the way nature intended, and often the first generation of man-made improvements must yield to the hydro generation.

So it was for the Miena pub. It was Amy's social centre for a significant part of her life, and the gathering point for a lot of isolated people. It was the nearest thing to a social life available to lonely people in lonely jobs. But the Hydro wanted to add some height to a nearby dam wall and the new backup of water would flood a lot of new country, including, so said the experts, the Miena pub. Water would come to its steps. It would be isolated, marooned. It would have to go.

So it went, and a part of life went with it for Amy and the others. They watched its demolition, mourned the pile of debris and memories that remained, and watched as the waters rose. But Government, of course, had got it wrong again. The pub site remained high and dry, as the pub would have been.

Amy had lost more than a regular night out: she had a couple of jobs at the Miena pub, waitress and barmaid. The money was handy to supplement the lean earnings from shepherding, and the meaning of those nights of warmth and cheer was more than money could buy.

'There was nothing like a Friday, Saturday night to get into the bar: the women were allowed in as well as the men, and many a morning it was breaking daylight when we decided to close the bar. We've got nothing at all in the Lake Country now.'

LOSERS ▲

▲ A BIG COUNTRY

Nothing but the inexorable change of seasons that dictate the life of a shepherd: time to move the sheep up when the snow is gone and the new growth of spring promises life for another year. For some. But not for a treasured foal Amy missed, then found as a bloodied pulp by the side of a road, victim of some thoughtless fool in a truck who'd come too fast over a crest in a road too narrow for both truck and young horse: the truck was bigger and faster. Amy paced out the trail of blood, nearly sixty metres the foal had been dragged. It would win no more prizes at Glenorchy Show or Tunbridge Fair. Amy had lost again.

A Big Country left her at that point. The rest of her story is an unhappy post-script.

Once, in this remote country, she had only to contend with nature, and some years that was bad enough, but progress was bringing new perils. The trek to and from the high country now had to run the gauntlet of roads and trucks and tourists' cars. Even the shepherd faced risks and, again, Amy lost. Herself victim of a road accident, she lost independent movement. She was made paraplegic. No more high country, no more shepherding.

She would stay in the Lake Country, Amy had told *A Big Country*, until the day they carried her out. But she hadn't meant it the way it had turned out. To be carried out was final, the end. But to have to be carried *about*... For a fiercely independent woman like Amy, that was another kind of end.

No Life in Simpson

'It sort of changes you, living in Simpson.'

Wendy speaking, a resident of a sad town in western Victoria named in tribute to the war hero, the man with the donkey at Gallipoli. But there's nothing heroic about Simpson, and very little that's even hopeful, because Simpson is a town whose only industry is welfare, and few people live there by choice.

Wendy has lived there since the time before welfare, when the Housing Commission township offered low-income earners their best chance, maybe their only chance, of achieving stage one of the Australian dream, a house which one day, if they kept up the payments for thirty or forty years, would be their own. Now she's not sure she wants to own the house that's been home for seventeen years because, to her, the character of the town has changed very much for the worse.

Two women told the story of Simpson to *A Big Country*: two women who did not know each other then and probably do not know each other still, such is the social division of the town. Wendy told the story of the long-term resident, with a stake in Simpson. Jenny told the story of the newcomer, the lone parent with nothing but welfare between her family and destitution. Separately and together, their stories are a contemporary Australian tragedy.

Things looked good for Simpson in those optimistic days of the 1960s when the town was built. All around was prosperous dairy country, and the butter and cheese factory was doing so well the Housing Commission built the township to accommodate all

SIMPSON'S NEAT HOUSING ESTATE, BUILT FOR THE WORKERS WHO NEVER CAME.
KEN STEPNELL

135

▲ A BIG COUNTRY

OPPOSITE PAGE: *Main Street, Simpson, Victoria: 'The reality of what could be the future for many country towns.'*

the new workers who would soon arrive. What arrived instead was the recession and whereas in other places the recession passed, in Simpson it became a permanent local depression.

Then the British joined the Common Market and dropped the trapdoor from under the export dairy market. Any future Simpson might have had was gone. But the new houses were there. No point in offering them to people who needed work as well as housing. It made good economic sense to offer them to people whose income was from welfare. That meant mainly single-parent families facing long waits for government housing in the city. The move to Simpson was, for many of them, a process of dumping.

That's how the established locals came to see it, too: their town was a dumping ground for city failures. Their property values slumped. They were stuck in Simpson as effectively as the newcomers they were beginning to resent.

Wendy felt herself becoming judgmental and knew it was wrong because she had always felt no-one had the right to judge another. 'But it sort of changes you, living in Simpson. After a while, your easy-going personality is gone. You become very hard, very cynical and at times you set yourself up as a judge.'

Under judgment are the single mothers, the deserted wives, the ones who got the blank tickets in the social draw of the Lucky Country.

The people we're concerned about are the people who seem to have given up on life. All they're concerned about is getting handouts. A lot of them have two pension cheques coming into the house, you can't say they're hard-up because they're probably getting more money than the average wage earner. Everything we've built here on this little block we've had to really earn and battle to get together . . .

LOSERS ▲

▲ A BIG COUNTRY

And the resentment mounts: aggrieved by the fear of loss of both communality and financial investment, Simpson's mortgage belt glares at the impoverished newcomers. The newcomers sense the hostility, and draw in upon themselves even further, grow even more unhappy, feel a despair that grows upon itself. Jenny says:

> *You have to explain yourself to so many people and you feel that you have this constant debt that you have to repay. I feel I always have to prove to people that I'm not a down-and-outer, that I'm trying as hard as I can to survive and to raise my son to be a worthwhile person. These days it's not so much a crime to be poor, but it is a crime to be poor and proud.*

Simpson was an aspect of *A Big Country* that showed the readiness of the changing group of program-makers to dive into deep social waters. The story was a landmark for the program and, unusually, the script allowed the luxury of editorial comment and a prediction:

> *There seem to be no answers in this town, everyone is a victim. For those like Jenny in the hands of an insensitive and uncaring system, Simpson is the reality of what could be the future for many Australian country towns. They have become the new battlers. As industry declines in country areas and pressures mount for public housing in crowded cities, the pattern will develop.*

A Trade in Bodies

If Simpson's direct warning of the development of a country town society characterised by deprivation should be ignored, it will be another example of the Australian genius for short-term thinking, of the national ability to create a problem where no problem previously existed. Out of sight, out of mind, is a motto not entirely unknown in Australia, and a past tendency towards the selective teaching of history has left many Australians with a distorted picture of the way things once were.

In this reporter's experience, as the saying goes, there are the convict record books at Port Arthur, Tasmania, from which whole pages have been neatly cut, and the etchings in a North Queensland library of hunting on the Atherton Tableland, hunting in which the quarry were human beings but, as black beings, considered at the time something less than human. The etchings, when requested for use in a television program, were found, strangely, to be missing.

While the northern gentry spent their weekends enjoying the stimulus of the hunt, some of their working time was spent worrying about where to find the labour to work the new sugar fields they were planning. The convict era had been brought to an end and European freemen were showing marked disinclination to work like slaves in the tropical sun.

Slaves!

Why not? It had worked well in America: the cotton, sugar and tobacco fortunes of the South were based on slavery. There were islands not far to Queensland's north full of blacks. Find a ship

Sugar cane and island woman: traces of Australia's slave trade.

▲ A BIG COUNTRY

OPPOSITE PAGE: *'SIXTY THOUSAND EMBARRASSING REMINDERS OF FORTY YEARS OF THE AUSTRALIAN SLAVE TRADE.' WHEN THE EMBARRASSMENT PROVED TOO MUCH, THE SLAVES WERE REPATRIATED. OR RATHER, SHIP OWNERS WERE PAID TO REMOVE THEM, JUST AS THEY'D BEEN PAID TO BRING THEM.*
NATIONAL LIBRARY OF AUSTRALIA

or two, recruit a crew of thugs, offer a bonus per head delivered alive, and there's the workforce. And so the slavers sailed to the Solomon Islands and to the New Hebrides. If recruiting failed, able-bodied men were tricked aboard and slammed in the holds, and only the relatively short voyages from the islands to the slave buyers saved the trade from the hideous mortality of the African slave traffic to America. The price per head, delivered to the Queensland port nearest the buyer's plantation, was £27.

It is rarely called slavery in Australian history books. We prefer to call it blackbirding, the faintly contemptuous term coined partly to disguise the existence of a slave trade. It is only one extended lifetime ago since the trade was outlawed and stopped. That was in 1901, when slavery was one thing the new Federation didn't want, despite the howls of protest from the Queensland sugar trade. Nor did the Federation want, as citizens, the slaves the traders had brought from Malaita, Guadalcanal, Tanna and Espiritu Santo: 60 000 embarrassing reminders of forty years of slave trading. The decision was made. They would be deported, and the chapter would be closed.

Many of them were sent back to the islands. Sometimes to the wrong island, but that didn't worry the shippers. A black was a black, and payment was per head, returned. If the books balanced and the passage was paid, what matter that a Malaita man from the Solomons was dumped on a beach in the New Hebrides among people who would very probably kill him.

Some stayed in Australia, graciously permitted to live on in the country which had sapped their working lives, for what were described at the time as 'compassionate reasons'. But there were conditions to the Government's kindness: the only work the ex-slaves, the kanakas, knew was work in the sugar fields,

LOSERS ▲

and this they were expressly forbidden to do.

The trade unions, flexing their new-found muscle, imposed a literal Black Ban: blacks were not to work as farm labourers, nor as anything else, for that matter, that might compete with the white man. The freed slaves found what scraps of land they could and became subsistence farmers. Their descendants, five generations on, live still outside the Australian society, further outside it than Aborigines or the islanders of Torres Strait.

They are deeply traditional people and some of the gardens established by their forebears more than eighty years ago still grow the taro that was their basic food. There are around 10 000 descendants of the sugar slaves living along the Queensland coast now. In white eyes, they share the prejudice against Aboriginals and Torres Strait Islanders, but they receive no share in the handouts the white Government provides for other black communities. They are made to feel on their own, they have always been made to feel that way, and the result has been the development of a proud and self-contained family, ten thousand strong. They are enthusiastic Christians, but underlying the beliefs of some, if not most, are the preserved traditions, beliefs and mysteries of their island origins.

Noel Fatnowna, whose ancestors were blackbirded from the Solomons, is a Queensland ambulance officer. His humour is rich in self-mockery:

> *Man, look at me today: white shirt, black epaulettes, a red band around my hat, saving people. When my grandfather came to this country he was a head-hunter, he was eating people, fighting and eating people in the Solomon Islands. And he ate 'em here too, Chinese. They reckon they were good, they were long pig, they made good soup.*

Noel Fatnowna gave his sons to Christianity, they weren't taught the beliefs of the old people. But now he has grandchildren, and they will be taught the old ways, he says, and Christianity as well.

There would appear, up on the hill there, two eagles, and they would fly direct from Guadalcanal, the Solomon Islands, to this place and they would bring messages of grief or messages of something to the old people. And a man's body might be in this place here, but his spirit would be in the Solomon Islands. He would transport himself through the sky, and they would go back if there was any sorrow or joy or anything they wanted to know. Some people say Black Magic, but no. It's a real thing. People say, 'We don't believe that, that's childish, silly talk,' but no, brother, that's the thing belonging to the black man. It's strength for him and he hangs on to it. That's his custom. That's his heritage. Today we say we don't hang on to it because of Christianity but it's inside of you so much that how can you forget?

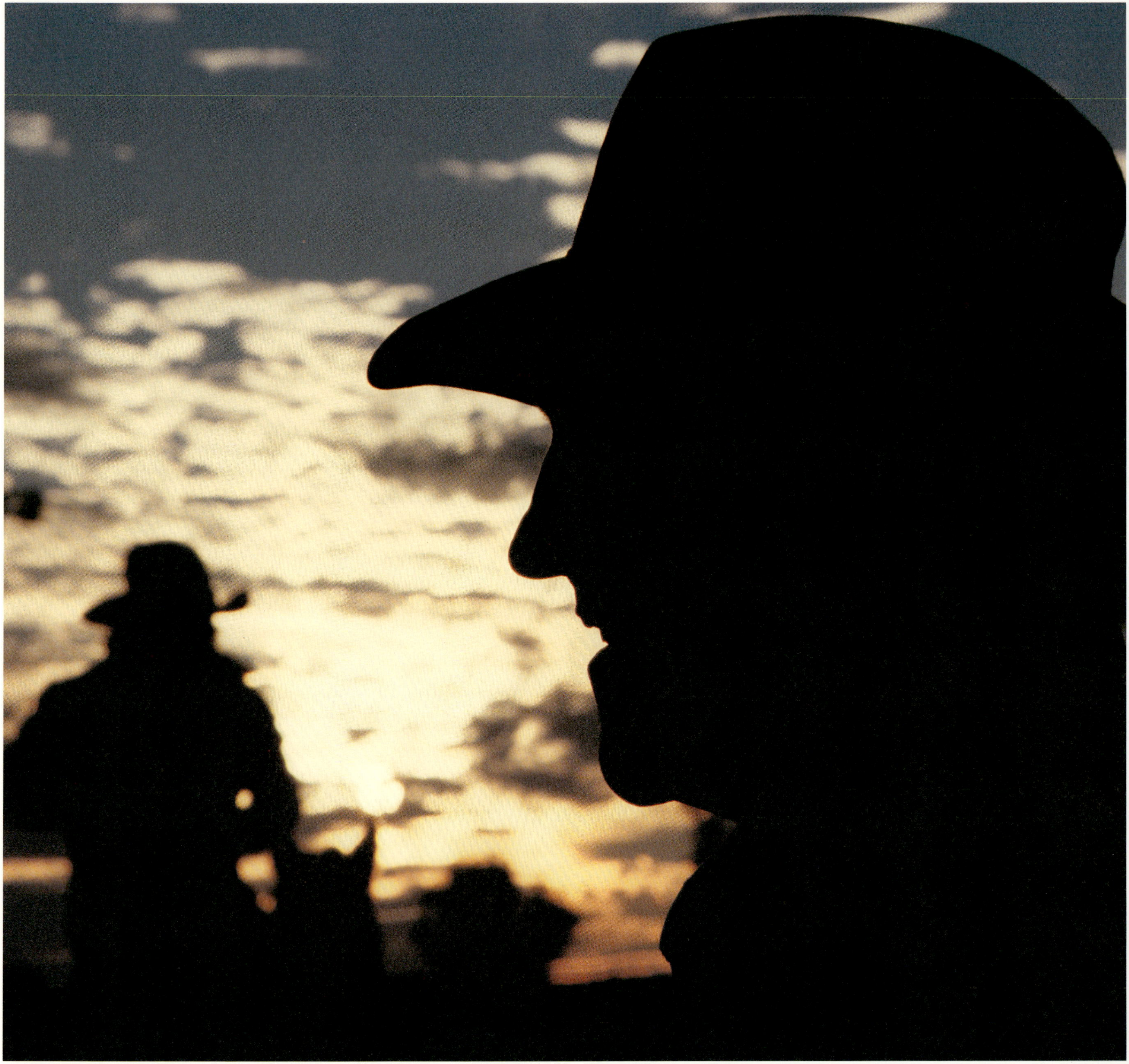

Winners

THE FOUR HORSEMEN of the Apocalypse, if riding in Australia, could well find their rank joined by a fifth. He would ride a spavined, sway-backed, stumbling horse, happiest when standing still or moving slowly backwards. He would be called The System, and resisting him has long been an Australian preoccupation.

Sometimes people who beat The System become very rich. Sometimes quite famous. And sometimes they're invited, or tempted, to ride pillion and to become themselves part of what they've been fighting. More often, though, a winner who has challenged The System successfully will return to relative obscurity, rewarded by the knowledge that because of what he or she did, something is different, something has changed.

The System exists in many forms: it can be a bureaucracy, a corporation, a military, a hostile city or a threat to a unique work of nature. All of these produced Winners who made their mark on the life of A Big Country.

OPPOSITE PAGE:
Drovers at Sunset.
KATHIE ATKINSON

One That Got Away

Edgardo Simoni was a winner by nature, and that made him an unhappy member of a losing army. Lieutenant Simoni was a professional soldier and no matter what the world thought of its obese and strutting leadership, he considered himself a member of a professional army, a descendant of the Legions of Rome. Doubly galling, then, to be ordered to surrender to amateurs, men who dressed untidily, moved sloppily, took orders grudgingly, and addressed as 'Tony' all their Italian captives in North Africa, officer and common soldier alike.

In the makeshift prison camp near the lost battlefield of Bardia, Simoni and the other 18 000 captive Italians learned they were to be shipped to Australia, Orzatrylia most of them called it, the home of these barbarians in shabby khaki and cowboy hats. At age twenty-four, the organised war of Edgardo Simoni ended and his personal, private war began. 'I wanted to get free, out of the fence. Any how. You have to escape, you must be, may be, the only one, but you must be the one who is able to escape.'

Simoni was able to escape, not once, but repeatedly. He was a folk hero to the interned Italian population of Australia, and a continuing embarrassment to the military whose incompetence he proved, first by escaping, then by being impossible to catch. He was out only overnight the first time, from the Murchison Prisoner-of-War camp in Victoria. But next time he was free for ten months. He lived in and from the bush. He learned something of the bush through the teacher Experience, and he came to love it.

EDGARDO SIMONI

▲ A BIG COUNTRY

OPPOSITE PAGE: *BARRED DOORS OF THE ONE TIME MILITARY STOCKADE AT HAY, NSW, FRAME THEIR MOST CELEBRATED PRISONER AS EDGARDO SIMONI RETURNS, VOLUNTARILY, TO THE BATTLEFIELD OF HIS PRIVATE WAR.*

A love of the bush of this strange country was all very well, but Simoni, by escaping, had done only part of what he saw as his military duty. It would not be complete until he returned home, to Italy, to report to his superiors that he, Edgardo Simoni, was the one, the only one, who had escaped. That meant he must make his way to the sea, to Melbourne, to seek the help of other Italians whose internment still allowed them a near-normal life, and to find a neutral ship for home.

Already, those in the Italian community who knew Simoni, or knew of him, were calling him La Volpe, The Fox, and at his foxiest, in Melbourne, Simoni took a job, not as something hidden and out of the way, but as a door-to-door salesman calling himself George Scotto, and trading on his considerable charm selling cosmetics to the ladies of suburban Melbourne.

He did very well at it and his employer, the Watkins Company, named him Salesman of the Month for his second month on the job. Then, without explanation, the star salesman left. The Fox had scented the breeze and found it hostile. Ahead of his pursuers, he went bush, but not far enough ahead this time, and he was caught.

In glee, the Australian military cast Simoni into what served as the Darkest Dungeon Australia had: the military stockade at Hay, in the west of New South Wales. It was to Hay, thirty-five years later, that Simoni returned, with *A Big Country* film crew to live again his darkest hour and greatest triumph.

'Okay Simoni,' they said, 'we'll send you to Hay. Top security jail. You won't get out of there.' Change the uniforms, add a German accent, and the scene parallels a Britisher on the way to Colditz. Hay and Colditz also had this in common: neither was escape proof.

WINNERS ▲

▲ A BIG COUNTRY

OPPOSITE PAGE, LEFT TOP AND BOTTOM: *PRISONER OF WAR (ITALIAN) NO. 47149.*

RIGHT: *FORTY YEARS ON, EDGARDO SIMONI WALKS AGAIN THE BANKS OF THE 'BIDGEE INTO THE FOREIGN AND ONCE HOSTILE BUSH HE BEFRIENDED, A TIME HE RECALLED AS 'JUST ME, THE RIVER AND THE SILENCE'.*

I had a lot of tricks [Simoni recalls]*, and I started planning as soon as I arrived here. I had to find the position first, where I was. I didn't know it. But I found that Hay was on the Murrumbidgee. The Murrumbidgee flows down to the Murray. On the Murray there is Mildura. I have a lot of friends there and so I say to myself, Okay, you'll be able to escape, to arrive to the river and then to the river at Mildura.*

Five months it took The Fox to prepare his escape from Hay stockade. Five months of mental and physical preparation. Five months of dieting to the edge of starvation to simulate life with no food while on the run. Five months infuriating prisoners in adjoining cells with his penetrating and toneless singing. Simoni had to sing. It was the only sound he could make to cover the noise of his stolen file scraping away at the bars of his cell, night after night for thirty nights. And he stole some white soap. He needed that to cover the file cuts in the white steel bars.

'It's a Lovely Day Tomorrow' he recalls was one of his most repeated songs. He relished the double purpose: the noise to cover the filing, and the words holding promise of his day of freedom.

On a summer night in 1943, he was ready. He rigged a dummy in his bed, left a cheerio note and ten shillings for his jailers 'to have a beer' and vanished into his familiar bush. Simoni fled into the parched heat of a summer drought. Ahead of him lay nearly 500 kilometres of doubly hostile country before he could expect to find friends. For nature was on the side of the enemy. Soldiers, police, bloodhounds and blacktrackers pursued him and the vast protective bush of his earlier escape was changed by drought to a vast and revealing bareness. Simoni knew the military wanted him back, but how important he was to them even his consider-

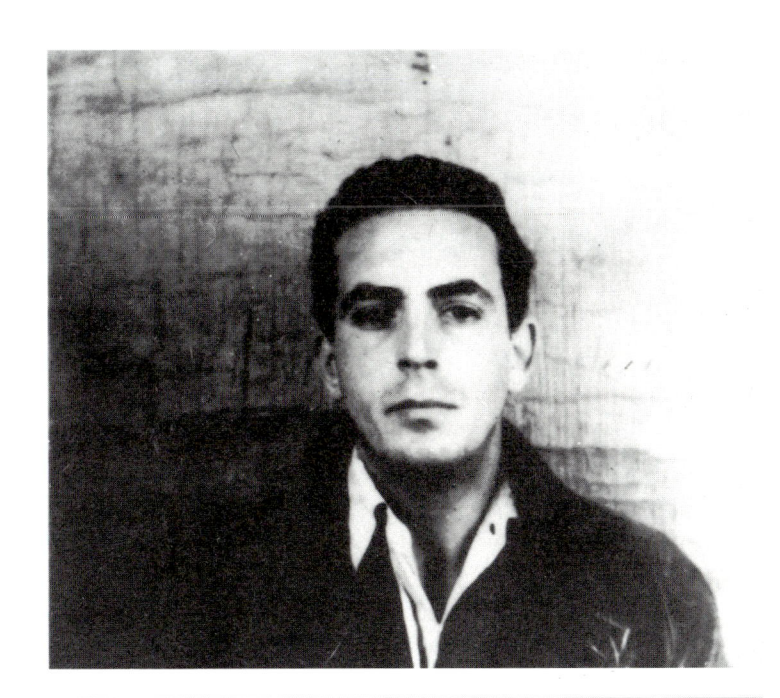

WINNERS ▲

able pride underestimated. For the inability of the military to hold one Italian prisoner reflected on more widespread military inadequacies. Reputations were at stake, promotions, even public esteem.

'Stop dreaming now, my boy,' Simoni urged himself. 'You've got to be shrewd and tricky. They are after you, they are chasing you. You've got to find food, swim across the river to and fro to hide your tracks. It will be hard, but you must do it.'

He learned some of the tricks of his namesake, The Fox, and alone and terribly isolated he began to play dangerous games with his pursuers, hiding in treetops and watching the search parties ride beneath him. Then he would wait until dark and creep into their camps to steal their food. Emboldened by his success, he stole a rowboat and set off downstream in more style and comfort than he'd known for weeks.

That was almost his undoing, for a policeman riding along the river bank saw him and knew or guessed who he was. The policeman had a rifle, and showed every sign of willingness to use it. A shouted interrogation of the boatman in mid-stream failed to convince the policeman that Simoni was the innocent Greek he claimed to be, and the rifle seemed ready to enter the argument. But Simoni had had a lot of dealings with Australians and he thought he knew their character. He staked his life on the belief than an Australian policeman wouldn't shoot an unarmed man whose only crimes were to lose a war and make fools of the military. Simoni was right. The policeman watched him row his boat to the far bank of the river and vanish into the bush.

Hunted and hungry, famished and occasionally ill, lonely beyond description, Edgardo Simoni found he was strangely, illogically happy. 'I could say "captured", yes, spellbound, spellbound by the river and the world around here. The remoteness of it, the stillness, to be alone here. I was happy, really happy, forgetting everything else, a different life, a different self. No running, no escaping, no guards. Just me, the river and the silence.'

Though it marked him for life, and left him with memories he would never forget, the bush failed to seduce Simoni or to divert him from the path of escape. After the brush with the river bank policeman, Simoni revised his plans and, rather than continue on for Mildura and the shelter of Italian friends, he turned south towards Bendigo, where he knew he could get a train to Melbourne, the sea and a neutral ship home.

Fifty-nine days and nearly 970 kilometres from Hay stockade, Simoni reached Melbourne, relaxed and confident and sure of his ability to hide among people, 'like a fish in the sea'.

Too relaxed, too confident, too sure. Filling in time waiting for a train, Simoni went walking in the pre-dawn morning in a Melbourne park. 'Suspicious' thought a young police patrolman, Bill Clottu, and his was the arm of the law which ended the saga and, for a while, the freedom of Edgardo Simoni.

The two met again when *A Big Country* filmed Simoni's sentimental return to Australia, and they laughed about the early morning meeting which had the policeman sitting on Simoni's chest to hold him until more police arrived. Cheeky to the end, 'Gee you're lucky' Simoni said to PC Clottu.

Thirty-five years on, and back in Australia, Simoni wanted to meet again the Italian friends who had harboured him and the Australian bush which had sheltered him in that great adventure of his young life. The friends, like Simoni himself, had aged, but the bush he found was ageless and the mark it had put on

▲ A BIG COUNTRY

him was there, unfaded, after half a lifetime. He went back to the Hay stockade, where a wall plaque records his escape and his one-time cell is a museum of tribute to the one who got away. And he went back to the Murrumbidgee bush and listened again to its subtle message:

> *I had to come back, some time, because I thought maybe it was a dream, just because you were a young man, free and getting so enthusiastic for life. Maybe that was the reason I felt so much for this time in the bush. But now that I come here again, I march in the same silence. I think that was poetical, sentimental if you want, but true, true.*
>
> *I'd like that many people, many men, could feel the same way in some moment of their lives. Free. Free into nature.*

Truchanas

Upstream, they had used a bulldozer to throw up a temporary dam. A man was missing in the rushing, tea-coloured water of Tasmania's Gordon River. Hopes for his life were gone. The search now was for his body. The makeshift dam slowed the rush of the wild Gordon and for a while the waters receded. Chance decided that it would be a close friend who would be first to see the sandshoe break the surface, and to realise its wearer was there, too, wedged dead in the branches of a submerged tree. The friend, more than a friend, for the dead man had been something close to a father, turned and walked away, and left it to others to recover the body of Olegas Truchanas.

There should have ended the story of one of the most remarkable men ever to adopt Australia as his home. As the Italian soldier Simoni had come unwillingly, a prisoner, in the best traditions of Australian settlement, Truchanas came voluntarily. Perhaps voluntarily is too positive a word. Desperately might be better, for Truchanas had to find somewhere to go. His country had been handed to its enemies in the aftermath of World War II. He was, in the language of the times, a Displaced Person. That was the official phrase for them. Australians had other words for the first wave of post-war immigrants: they were Balts or Poles, refugees from the Baltic States or from Poland, where the goose-stepping jackboots of temporary German overlords had been replaced by the goose-stepping jackboots of Russian overlords whose occupation was to last much, much longer.

OLEGAS TRUCHANAS,
A LAST PORTRAIT.
RALPH HOPE-JOHNSTONE

▲ A BIG COUNTRY

OPPOSITE PAGE: *GONE, NEVER TO BE SEEN AGAIN, THE EXQUISITE LAKE PEDDER, TASMANIA, PHOTOGRAPHED BY OLEGAS TRUCHANAS BEFORE IT WAS COVERED BY A HYDRO-ELECTRIC STORAGE DAM.*
OLEGAS TRUCHANAS

Olegas Truchanas, then, was a Balt, a Lithuanian, a small-town boy turned resistance fighter against the Germans but tasting in victory only the gall of Russian occupation. He fled to Bavaria then, by the tortuous processes of the time, sought to migrate to Australia. He could come, he was told, along with scores of thousands of others, but to show due gratitude to the generosity of the Australian immigration system, he must agree to work where, and at what, the nabobs of the immigration system decreed. It was the age of doctor turned labourer, merchant made navvy, teacher taught to work on the roads. Some people that system ruined. Others it made, by forcing them to change in mid-life the direction they were heading.

Olegas Truchanas, the Balt with the strange name, was put to work as a labourer at the zinc refinery near Hobart. To escape a hideous working environment, he took to the bush at weekends, drawing on boyhood hikes and resistance experience of living off the land to sustain him in exploration of his new world. He was a loner, and he trekked alone. The territory he chose to explore was one of the last wilderness areas of the world, Tasmania's unknown south-west, and the realisation that he was going where perhaps no man had gone before thrilled him. On holiday he would disappear for weeks at a time, and bring back photographs of what he had seen.

He climbed the south-west's highest mountain, Federation Peak, alone and without the trappings of climbing others had used. He canoed the fiercest river, the Gordon, whose length no-one had traversed before, and on his second attempt he followed that wild river from its source to the sea. He found that the details of maps of the area were often wrong, and he drew new ones. At the end of his epic journey down the Gordon, he tied up his canoe in calm water at Macquarie

WINNERS ▲

▲ *A BIG COUNTRY*

Harbour and went looking for a telephone to call his wife in Hobart. There were those who would not believe he had done it, but he had photographs of where he had been, photographs of country no European had seen before.

Truchanas had made the wilderness both his love and his work. He had gone to work for the Hydro-Electric Commission, Tasmania's Government-within-Government, as an engineering assistant. In his vacations he repeatedly returned to the southwest. He used cameras and film to record his impressions, but what emerged were more than photographs, and though achieved by standard photographic chemical means, they had the quality of paintings. His years of exploration yielded a collection of many thousands of photographs, a unique record of an unknown wilderness.

All were destroyed in a few minutes by another force of the nature, bushfire. Among the 1500 homes destroyed in south-east Tasmania in the great fire of 1967 was the Truchanas' family home and everything in it.

'I feel,' he told a friend, the artist Max Angus, at the time, 'my whole life's work has been in vain.'

His life's work, in fact, was about to begin: the Tasmanian Government announced that as part of the search for ever more hydro-electricity, the exquisitely beautiful Lake Pedder would be flooded to make a storage pond, drowned under fifteen metres of water. The lake, a mountain jewel with a beach of bright white quartz sand, would be gone forever.

Truchanas found himself in an intolerable position. He was working for the organisation which was threatening to destroy a place that he loved more than most, a place his explorations, his photographs, had brought to a wider world of nature lovers. His criticism was gagged, by public service rules used often in Aus-

OPPOSITE PAGE:
THE TRUCHANAS VIEW OF A NATIONAL TREASURE UNDER THREAT—THE ORIGINAL LAKE PEDDER, LOOKING TOWARD THE FRANKLAND RANGE. HIS PICTURES ARE AN ELOQUENT ARGUMENT FOR CONSERVATION.
OLEGAS TRUCHANAS

▲ A BIG COUNTRY

OPPOSITE PAGE:
Mountains, mists and lakes: across the valley of the original Lake Pedder to Mt Anne.
OLEGAS TRUCHANAS

tralia to stifle informed comment on contentious affairs. He was not allowed to speak out about Lake Pedder, nor to write. But there was a gap in public service thinking: no-one had thought to ban photographs, and from the cameras of Olegas Truchanas came an eloquent plea for conservation of one of the little treasures of the world.

It failed, of course. History has shown that only very big guns can resist the power of the Hydro-Electric Commission, but one man and his photographs could and did show the world what was being lost. Truchanas set out to photograph Lake Pedder in all its moods, confiding to his friend Max Angus that the battle was lost and a new battle was about to begin. Truchanas knew the planning schedule of the Hydro. He knew that lines were already being drawn on maps in preparation for the damming of the last wild river, the Gordon. And he knew that such a dam would destroy more than a wilderness river: it would provide access to the last great stand of Huon pine trees in the world, and trees that had lasted a thousand years would fall in months to the greed of loggers.

He knew something by now of the ways of Government, and he knew an increasingly powerful conservation movement was sweeping through ring-bark-and-axe-happy Australia. Truchanas succeeded in having the Huon pines declared a reserve, off-limits to hard men with chain saws in their hands and their bosses with woodchip orders in their pockets. That battle won, he concentrated again on saving the Gordon River from death by damming, and he decided one more detailed exploration and photographing trip was necessary. He was tired to near exhaustion, strained physically and emotionally and stressed to his limit. Family and friends thought it was not the time to begin a dangerous journey down a treacherous river, alone, as always, but the man had work to do.

WINNERS ▲

▲ A BIG COUNTRY

They found his canoe first, torn open along half its length, and then when the bulldozer had made a temporary dam and the water level fell, they brought back the body of the Man of the Wilderness. His friends selected from his pictures taken since the fire, and presented his story in a book. It was a best seller. It brought the wilderness to the world, it made the Gordon River a national cause, and it helped stay the hand of mindless development. Olegas Truchanas had left his priceless legacy.

The Kid Who Failed Sunday School

Not many kids fail Sunday school. Don Shand did.

Such lack of promise didn't affect his life all that much: he was a company chairman in his early forties, a leader, a survivor, an innovator, in the cannibalistic world of Australian commercial aviation. He had a hand in the foundation of East-West, long a burr under the comfortable saddle of the two-airline duopoly and, as the airline's chairman for a quarter of century, kept it safe from the marauders who coveted its success and feared its potential.

He started early in business. His sister Millie told *A Big Country* of the day Don asked to borrow a couple of shillings, to go to Flemington market to buy a sheep. He sold the sheep to a butcher, at a profit, and bought more. The business career of Don Shand was on its way.

Later, working the land, he wondered why Americans could get three times the maize production from their land as Australian farmers. The land must be about the same, he reasoned, what about the seed? Thus came hybrid maize to Australia, and up went the yields. He had the crops. It was wartime, and he had the markets, feeding the military. But how to get the crops from paddock to market, the army having soaked up the pool of farm labour? Don Shand organised a kind of Land Army, recruiting women in nearby towns and arranging buses to bring them to the farm. They worked 8 am to 5 pm, even brought their own lunches, and the idea was so good it became part of the national war effort. They even grew opium, needed to make medical drugs.

DON SHAND: A HEAD FOR BUSINESS AND A HEART FOR AEROPLANES.

▲ A BIG COUNTRY

OPPOSITE PAGE, TOP: An 'Aggie': known well but not altogether loved by 1940s bomber crew trainees, the Avro Anson was one of the war surplus aeroplanes that got East-West Airlines off the ground.
EAST-WEST AIRLINES

BOTTOM: The airline's independent existence lasted into the jet age of the Fokker F-28.
EAST-WEST AIRLINES

In the euphoria of the war's end and the flush of victory, some quite impossible ideas got off the ground in Australia. Impossible, because foreigners had always been quick to tell us they were impossible. But a time of threat, with the Japanese knife at the national throat, had caused Australians to doubt some of the earlier advice of foreign friends and, in the interests of survival, to attempt things long held impossible. Wackett and his aeroplanes; Hartnett and his field guns; the extraordinary effort which saw Australia create from nothing—first overcoming allied commercial opposition—an optical glass industry so that sights could be made for the guns Hartnett's factories were producing. In that garden of enterprise, which bloomed all too briefly, Don Shand got interested in aeroplanes.

War surplus planes, principally the C-47 Dakota workhorses, littered military airfields across Australia. Slap some seats in, some sound-deadener and decorative lining over the bare metal ribs and skin, call it DC-3, and you had the raw material for an airline. With Shand optimism, the fledgling short-haul line, licensed to fly mainly north-south routes within New South Wales, was named East-West, with unmistakably transcontinental meanings and intentions. The signals of future punch-ups were not lost on the opposition, and the business of shutting out East-West became an airline boardroom preoccupation that would continue for forty years without resolution.

Don Shand, meanwhile, went to America to look at the aviation business and came back with a new direction for his company: he made it the first crop-dusting outfit in Australia, spreading superphosphate from makeshift and fragile aeroplanes not intended as flying farmers.

He watched airline emphasis placed more and more on luring passengers into seats, and realised the direction was wrong. Freight was the future for air

WINNERS ▲

transport, he thought, as planes became bigger and faster, and airlines more and more numerous and competitive, and empty space on their flights more and more common. Why not, he asked, fill the space with freight, use the southern hemisphere's seasonal advantage of being back to front with the north, and supply the really big markets with the fresh produce of Australia? He'd done the sums: there were 600 tonnes of unused air-freight-space flying wastefully out of Australia every month.

Expensive though, surely, to fly an orange across the world?

He had worked that one out, too. He knew the retail price of off-season oranges in cities abroad, and there could have been profit in it. But it didn't happen and, as Don Shand put it, 'Once space is lost on an aeroplane, it's lost forever, and this country can't afford to lose any space at all on its aircraft going out.'

The planes of his own airline were doing well, the initial revenue of $16 000 a year had grown to seven million. Shand's goal was twenty million. Envious eyes were on East-West and the Chairman's job was to fight off the takeover tactics of the mighty Reg Ansett. Perhaps with an eye to Australia's future, Don Shand said he had no time for takeovers, he'd rather help another company to live and grow. He made a family fight of it and the tightly held shares and the proprietorial attitude of shareholders helped him stay independent.

Don Shand had gone before his airline became a traded commodity in the halls of business, though it flies further afield now than ever before. The name remains, but the airline today is a subsidiary of a big one.

One of its aeroplanes, a neat Dutch-built jet painted green and gold, has the old chairman's name on its nose, D M Shand. But the Sunday school register is long gone that might have recorded D M Shand, Failed.

Lights in the Valley

One of the holiest of words in the Australian political vocabulary is Decentralisation. Its dictionary meaning is clear cut: to transfer from the central. But in Polspeak, that unique language of those who aspire to lead us, it means Goodies for the Bush and, a notation might well add, goodies in the nature of promises that only sometimes ever happen.

In the early 1970s, at huge cost to the taxpayer, new bureaucracies were set up in Canberra and elsewhere to put some flesh around the bones of political promises to move some industry, some economic activity, out of the cities and into deserving country towns. Growth centres they were called, and the chosen included Albury-Wodonga and Bathurst-Orange. There was one in South Australia too, a phantom city in the Adelaide Hills that never became anything more than a signpost to good intentions.

Amid the hoo-ha and the floodgates of government money that poured wealth upon landholders lucky enough to have farmed land on the outskirts of the so-called growth centres (land that, more than a decade on, has yet to achieve its intended purpose) a Melbourne company quietly moved its operations to the bush. A decade on, the growth centre concept all but abandoned and no-one too keen to count the costs and the losses, the former Melbourne lighting-fittings maker Planet Products remains a happy and successful part of bush Australia.

Planet's Chairman, Jack Iggulden, decided to make the move, for all the right reasons. Something of a maverick in Australian busi-

JACK IGGULDEN, BUSINESS MAVERICK.

A BIG COUNTRY

OPPOSITE PAGE: *The Bellinger Valley, NSW: natural beauty but economic uncertainty.*
AUSTRAL INTERNATIONAL

ness terms, Iggulden had made loud conservationist noises in Melbourne, and went further than the average 'greenie'. In the vast Monopoly game that the development business became in Melbourne, he challenged in very direct ways the construction of a pipeline across Port Phillip Bay, and landed in the square marked Go To Jail. To jail he went for his conservationist beliefs.

Not surprisingly, he found himself increasingly soured by the pressures and tensions of an industrial city and he began to think of moving. The thought matured to intention, but move to where? This man thought big. The move, he knew, would be no more difficult whether it were ten miles or a thousand. He chose a thousand, and moved lock stock and family to Bellingen, in northern New South Wales. He had been looking for a place that was 'uncorrupted' and in Bellingen he thought he'd found it.

Planet Products came like a benign visitor from space to the sleepy town in the Bellinger Valley. Dairying and timber, its mainstays, were shaky, and the future was anybody's guess. Planet had left most of its former staff in Melbourne and suddenly in Bellingen there were sixty new jobs, thousands of dollars a week entering and merrily circulating in a starved local economy.

You would have thought they'd make him mayor, but all was not well in the relationship between this captain of local industry and the community he had adopted because with him from Melbourne, with the machines and the plans and the capital, Jack Iggulden had brought his conservationist beliefs and the things he saw going on around his new home appalled and angered him.

One hundred years ago, the forests of northern New South Wales appeared inexhaustible and were harvested in that belief without any attempt to replace them. In four or five generations, the timber was cut out. At the time of Jack

WINNERS ▲

▲ *A BIG COUNTRY*

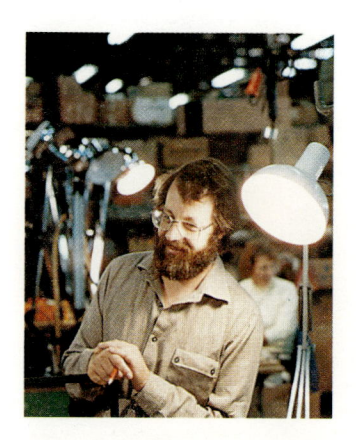

Iggulden's arrival in the Bellinger Valley, the argument was hotting up about the fate of the few good trees that remained. Iggulden, naturally, was on the side of conservation, and that put him firmly on one side of a very clear local divide—the old story of a thousand communities, the old against the new. The difference in the Bellinger Valley was that the newcomers were for conservation while the longer-term residents, with timber-getting in their blood and their traditions as well as their wallets, wanted no interference with their freedom to cut what and where they willed. And there was another factor: the locals didn't think much of many of the newcomers. They wore their hair long, and strange clothes, and, if you could believe rumour, smoked and drank strange things and behaved in private in ways of which the locals did not approve. Agree with them, Jack Iggulden found, on matters of conservation, and you might as well be one of them according to local opinion.

He had expected more of a country town when he made the move from the city: he thought there would be unity in a small community, that the divisions increasingly characteristic of city societies would not exist. They did exist, he found, and perhaps even more strongly because, lacking the anonymity of a city, the battle lines of opposing beliefs were all the clearer to see.

Not much point, he found, in arguing that the conservation movement was not the enemy of timber men whose jobs were threatened. History was the enemy, all the trees were gone; only the scraps remained and they would be gone, too, in a year or three or five. Only in conservation could there be any future for the timber industry. But the irony of that proposition was lost in immediate economic pressures.

So the old 'greenie' withdrew, to his own personal piece of environment in

ABOVE: *Brett Iggulden: production management in Paradise.*

OPPOSITE PAGE: *At Bellingen, NSW, the private decentralisation project of Planet Products, once of Melbourne, has more the air of a country club than a factory. But a factory it is, and a successful one.*

170

WINNERS ▲

the Bellinger Valley, to an idea he had had when the move from the city changed from an idea to an intention to a plan: 'I will surround myself with my own environment which nobody will bugger up in my lifetime, enough space around me in which I can live without the disturbance all the time of seeing the environment degraded.'

And the business? Doing nicely, by all accounts, and expanding. Staffed by people, the managers say, who care about what they do and are quietly proud to slap on the boxes of product they send away stickers saying 'Made In Bellingen'.

Taking On the System

The conservation movement in Australia came of age in the 'seventies: Jack Mundey and his Builders Labourers' Green Bans preserved the face of parts of old Sydney; Bob Brown in Tasmania took on the might of the Hydro-Electricity Commission and its beaver-like determination to build dams; and in Queensland, one man set out to preserve an island.

John Sinclair was an unlikely crusader. He could almost be called an Establishment Man. A member of the Queensland Country Party (now the National Party), he was a middle-class professional, a family man, moderately successful, happy and satisfied. But in the view of the Queensland establishment there was a flaw in this man. There were to him some places so precious, some values so important, some standards so immutable, that the pressures of commerce and their subservient politics were secondary. Above most things, John Sinclair loved Fraser Island.

It was a love he had inherited. His parents had honeymooned there half a century before when the only people who knew about Fraser Island were the locals in and around the nearest mainland town, Maryborough. Fraser is the biggest sand island in the world, 120 kilometres long, 1598 square kilometres in area, and although structured almost entirely of sand, supporting a rich and varied vegetation.

In its sands there are metals, rare and industrially valuable metals, zircon, rutile, ilmenite, which are in demand overseas to make paint pigments and, among other things, surgical implants

JOHN SINCLAIR: A 17-YEAR FIGHT FOR A CAUSE. NEWS LIMITED

▲ A BIG COUNTRY

OPPOSITE PAGE: *FRASER ISLAND, QUEENSLAND: SAVED FROM MINING, BUT TOURISM AND THE FOUR-WHEEL-DRIVE PRESENT NEW THREATS TO ITS DELICATE ECOLOGY.*
MIKE DOBEL/AUSTRAL-INTERNATIONAL

and parts of jet bombers. By 1971, two sand-mining companies were eating up the fragile dunes of Fraser Island at 1200 tonnes an hour, extracting the wanted minerals and leaving the rest, the droppings, or tailings in miner's language, where it lay. John Sinclair saw they were destroying Fraser Island and he set out to stop them. With a group of concerned conservationists, he found his political voice.

Maryborough. With wife and three sons, Sinclair was comfortably at home in this normally friendly, typically Queensland town. He had gone to its grammar school, as had his father and his father's father. He had become a lecturer in the adult education system, and had joined the ruling political party. His life seemed secure in a town where security was threatened. The one local industry, a shipyard, had closed and with it went hundreds of jobs. Stopgap measures were providing some work, but the town's hopes for new security rested on forestry and sand mining. Both involved Fraser Island. Both were the targets of the conservation movement which was determined to stop them. Town opinion and the conservationists were on collision course. John Sinclair, as the very visible leader of the 'greenies', found lined up against him not just the powers and publicists of the sand miners, but many of his old friends as well.

In a television commercial, the miners claimed titanium from Fraser Island was saving the lives of little children with faulty hearts. And so, no doubt, it was. But the glib admen failed to mention titanium's rather less humanitarian role in critical assemblies of the jet bombers which had recently rained down napalm and high explosive onto the little children of Vietnam.

In Maryborough, Queensland, John Sinclair found himself sent to Coventry. Community hatred was an experience new to him. It was new, too, to hear

WINNERS ▲

OPPOSITE PAGE, LEFT: *THE BIGGEST SAND ISLAND ON EARTH, AND HIDDEN IN THE SANDS OF FRASER ISLAND A TREASURY OF RARE METALS.*
LEO MEIER/ WELDON TRANNIES

RIGHT: *RAINFOREST SHOULDN'T GROW IN SAND, BUT NO ONE TOLD THAT TO FRASER ISLAND.*
WELDON TRANNIES

himself called 'radical' for his stand in defence of a natural wonder, and to hear the apparent security of his government job thrown against him and of the 'threat' he represented to the job security of others. Of a vote at a Maryborough public meeting in support of mining, Sinclair said: 'It's as stupid for these people to put their hands up in favour of "controlled" sand mining as it would be for the people of Alice Springs to vote to quarry Ayers Rock.' The comment did not improve his standing in Maryborough. What he had to say the town didn't want to hear.

This was not an issue that would be decided by the votes of orchestrated public meetings in a country town. The future of Fraser Island would be settled in court, and the Queensland court found in favour of mining. So did the Queensland Supreme Court, where the case went on appeal. But, argued elsewhere, in the High Court in Canberra, the Queensland decisions were turned around and, in May 1975, the highest court in the land ruled for conservation.

After six years of disputation, Fraser Island was an issue known far beyond Queensland. The national Government, persuaded it was a national issue, set up an inquiry of its own to decide if export licences for Fraser Island's minerals should be revoked. That was a Whitlam Government initiative, but the events of 11 November 1975 meant another leader, and another Government, would make the decision: Malcolm Fraser's decision was that mining should stop.

John Sinclair, the conservation campaigner, had won. But John Sinclair, the individual, was about to learn he had lost. He would feel all the pressures an outraged system could bring to bear.

He was voted Australian of the Year; the Queensland Government abolished his job in Maryborough.

He was a national figure; the first enforced move away from home began

WINNERS ▲

▲ *A BIG COUNTRY*

the process that would end his marriage.

He was a hero to conservationists everywhere; the Queensland Government, his employer, transferred him from job to job eight times.

He was a man who had fought for a belief and won.

His adversary, a Government of the people for the people, would neither forgive nor forget. Sinclair's life was made untenable.

Feeling, he says, like a political refugee and just as desperate, he crossed a border, alone, to begin a new life. He had been, he says, under personal siege for seventeen years. The saving of Fraser Island had cost him everything he had, family, home and job. Even his victory was less than complete, for having lost out on mining, the next covetous eyes cast on Fraser Island were those of loggers and over that the State Government had full control. The timber men moved in on the island's rainforests. And there was a bitter irony: the place had become so famous through Sinclair's campaigning that people wanted to see the island, to holiday there, and the tourist trade grew from the few familiar locals to a horde of 300 000 a year.

So much for the ideal of wilderness.

John Sinclair occasionally ventures north of that line on the map and goes quietly back to Fraser Island which draws him still as strongly as it ever did. Though it's a different island now, he says, the loggers have done ecological damage that will take thousands of years for nature to repair, and the scars of sand mining are there to disprove the miners' old claims of complete restoration. That, and the tourists, and the four-wheel-drives, and the trail bikes...

Was it worthwhile, taking on the system? It's the sort of thing people have gone to war about, John Sinclair says. Yes, Fraser Island was worth fighting for.

OPPOSITE PAGE:
SANDHILLS, FRASER ISLAND: THEIR PRESERVATION A TRIUMPH FOR ONE MAN'S DEDICATION.
OLIVER STREWE/WILDLIGHT

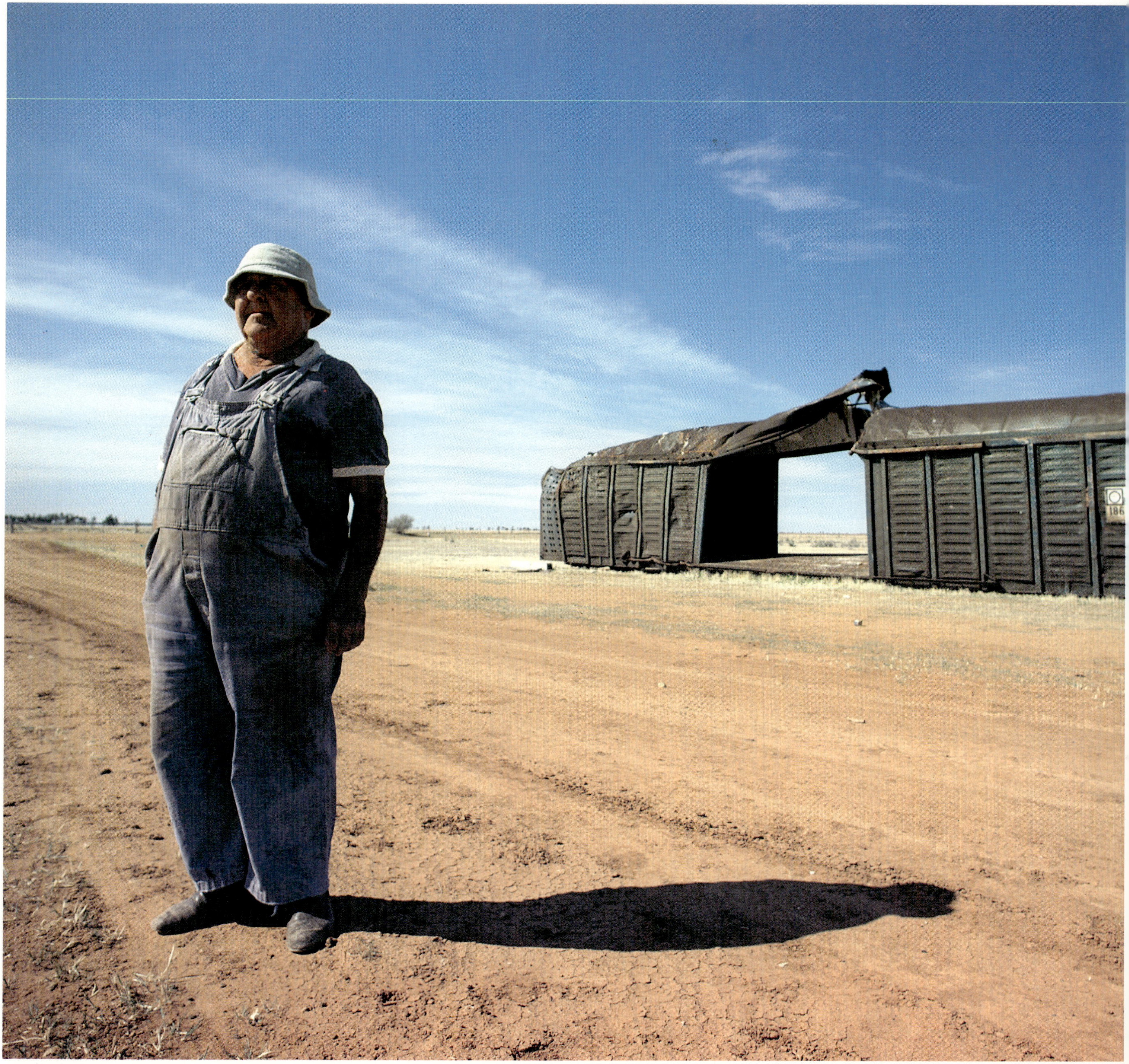

FACES, PLACES

THE TRUE ART of television is the ability to get people to tell their stories, to talk as they would to friends while an inquisitive near-stranger asks question after question and a thoroughly intimidating collection of picture and sound recorders is pointed at them. It is an art that the people who have worked for A Big Country over its two decades have practised with rare skill. Rarely were they given what they thought was enough time to do the job, almost never had they the luxury of a pre-filming visit to the people and places to be featured in the film. Most contacts were made by telephone, often by two-way radio. The success of so many of their efforts says as much for the imperturbable nature of the people filmed as it does about the talents of the film-makers.

People told their life stories, told of their triumphs and failures, successes and disappointments, their loves, their interests, their jobs. They made it possible for A Big Country to tell the stories of a natural-born politician from an island in Torres Strait; of an amateur drama production whose cast rehearsed by radio; of a man whose life's work was photographing beach girls; and of a couple of real-life romances, one of them between a Princess and a Canecutter.

OPPOSITE PAGE: BIG COUNTRY. BIG MAN. BIG PROBLEMS. FARMER, NSW.
COLIN BEARD/WELDON TRANNIES

The Princess and the Canecutter

The Murray Islands are part of Australia, but who has ever heard of them, and where are they? Go north in Australia as far as you can, till your feet splash into the warm aqua-blue water off the end of Cape York Peninsula and you're in Torres Strait. Find a canoe and head off east of north-east in the Coral Sea towards Port Moresby and, if you're an islander with a natural gyro-compass built into your senses, you will find the Murray Islands.

They are three, and they are small, the products of a long dead volcano. A proud and fierce and adventurous people settled them, people who lived by the rules of the god Mer and who were therefore called Meriams. They raided and plundered other islands. They hunted for heads, the gods alone knew what happened to the rest of the bodies of those they conquered. Always seamen, they became traders, the story of their race a later antipodean equivalent to that of the Vikings. Eight tribes shared the Murrays, and they prospered.

Bad luck that their paradise became the edge of a 1940s battlefield. Authority in Australia decided to evacuate the Murray Islanders and, with no doubt the best of intentions, to dump them in Brisbane. One exile was the first-born grand-daughter of Great Mamoos, a king in life and legend, and she was therefore what we would call a princess. But she was called just Polly, a girl about to become a woman, transplanted suddenly, without warning or understanding, into an utterly foreign and hostile city.

The childhood of the Island Princess Polly had been all that

POLLY ROMANO, GRAND-DAUGHTER OF AN ISLAND KING.

▲ A BIG COUNTRY

OPPOSITE PAGE: FROM MURRAY ISLAND, THE BROWN VIKINGS CALLED MERIAMS—SEAMEN, RAIDERS, TRADERS—ONCE DOMINATED THE ISLANDS BETWEEN AUSTRALIA AND NEW GUINEA.
WELDON TRANNIES

an island childhood is imagined to be. She lived in a home of happiness in a place of plenty, and shared the islanders' communion with the sea and its creatures, a relationship so close and so delicate that even sharks were playthings and children swam among them and pulled their tails. And just as her childhood was ending, her island life ended too, when the evacuation boat loaded every last Murray Islander aboard and sped off south ahead of the expected Japanese invasion. It would be more than half a lifetime before she would see her islands again.

Skip a few years. War over, Polly is grown up, living in the North Queensland sugar town, Ingham. Not a lot of social life in Ingham in the 'fifties, the local dance is the high spot of the week. From opposite ends of the earth there came one night to the Ingham dance hall The Princess and the Canecutter.

It would be hard to say who felt the more foreign, Polly from the Murray Islands or Frank Romano not long arrived from Italy. Frank cautiously looked around the dance hall, rigidly divided, males from females, as was the custom of the time and the place. Polly had noticed him from the time his head appeared at the door, once-over-ing the place before committing himself to enter. He was a bit short by island standards, she thought, when he asked her to dance. Thirty-some years and eight children later, Polly Romano cooks Italian mostly, Chinese sometimes, Island style hardly at all.

But she is on the way home, to the Murray Islands. After forty-three years the Princess returns. Both she and the Islands have greatly changed. Life has been happy but hard for Polly. For years, she joined Frank in the cane fields, cutting alongside him, maybe the first and only woman to do so. 'He cut three lines, I'd cut two. He cut four, I cut three. It's hard, hard work. Not a lady's life.'

They would joke that when they came home from work, the children

FACES, PLACES ▲

▲ A BIG COUNTRY

OPPOSITE PAGE, LEFT: *THE PRINCESS, POLLY* AND RIGHT: *THE CANECUTTER, FRANK ROMANO*

would think they were 'bogey-men'. They were all black from the burned cane and although Polly had a natural start, she and Frank were indistinguishably black at the end of a day in the cane fields. 'He was like me—all black.' She cut cane for six years.

Polly had seen early on that Frank Romano, though 'short by island standards', was a special man. Eight kids of his own in Australia to feed and clothe and educate, he also had family in Italy, living close to the bread line and needing his support to break, by education, the cycle of poverty. Frank financed younger brothers to the education he never had himself—he still cannot read nor write in either Italian or English. To support both families, he worked ten, twelve, sometimes fourteen hours a day. And weekends? What are weekends? A week has seven working days.

In 1975, Frank had an accident at work that left him crippled. His future, if he listened to the experts, was in a wheelchair. That prospect he wouldn't even consider. But the homeland was drawing him back: he could see a prospect of returning to Italy far better off than when he had left, maybe with enough money to buy some land, to be the farmer instead of the farmhand.

If he went to Italy, Polly would go too, but she wanted something else: she wanted to walk again on the crisp white beaches of her islands, see her people, speak again her own language. And in 1986, she did, and she allowed film-makers from *A Big Country* to record a return that was more sad than triumphant, because time had not been kind to the Murray Islands and their people. Polly found the eight tribes shrunk to just a couple of hundred people, the many villages reduced to one, the gods Mer and Malu and Waeit banished by the followers of a new faith, the once warrior race looking now to missionaries for spiritual and cultural

FACES, PLACES ▲

needs, and to government welfare for earthly necessities.

The experience left Polly saddened and confused. Now that she had returned, she was all the more aware of the old rule that you can't go back, and the feeling was strongly upon her that this would be the last time she would see her islands. The future for the Princess of the Murray Islands would be more of the recent past, as Mrs Romano, wife of Frank, core of a family of children and children's children, her island origin preserved only in memories of a time, a people, and a way of life that once she was privileged to share.

The Smartest Man on Darnley

By canoe, with a good wind and strong oarsmen, the Torres Strait Islands navigators would make fast passage from the Murrays to the neighbouring Darnley Island, first to raid, later to trade. These days, Darnley is the more important because it is the administrative centre of the Eastern Islands of the Strait. And it is the home of George Mye. George is no chief; no noble blood runs in his veins. He is not a traditional leader, a tribal patriarch. But he is the smartest man on Darnley Island. He's smart in Brisbane, too, when he goes there to tell a State Government what it ought to be doing in and for the Torres Strait Islands. And perhaps his greatest gift is that he's particularly smart in Canberra, and knows his way around its corridors and its egos.

One story best sums up George Mye: erosion was threatening to undermine the island church. 'A punishment from God,' the church leaders said, and they called for prayers. George Mye saw it was all down to high tides and winds. He called on Canberra for money, and built a retaining wall.

Darnley Island runs itself. A benign dictatorship extends some long-distance authority from Brisbane, but man can get to the moon in about the time it takes to get to Darnley, so effective control is local. That means it's George Mye. Group Representative of the Eastern Islands is his formal title. He must walk something of a tightrope, for though the real power is his, symbolic authority is held, by right of birth, by someone else and everyone must know and acknowledge that, George Mye included, if the fragile system is

GEORGE MYE OF DARNLEY ISLAND.
NEWS LIMITED

▲ A BIG COUNTRY

OPPOSITE PAGE: *DARNLEY ISLAND: SEEKING AN END TO THE 'PATERNAL GUIDANCE' FROM FAR-AWAY WHITE MEN.*
DOLPHINA BIN TAHAL

to work. That it does work says much for everyone concerned.

Darnley Island gave its name to the Darnley Deep, the notorious graveyard of pearl divers, where rich beds of pearl shell lured divers to go too deep and stay down too long and surface racked by that dreadful condition called The Bends, and too often to die of it as the luggers beat their way back to the nearest help at Thursday Island. George Mye was a diver, for trocus rather than pearls, but the shell industry collapsed and he found himself on the beach and looking for work. He took up teaching, then opened a shop. His real role in life, that of politician, came from an experience while working for the Queensland Government.

There was a bizarre row over a tombstone. Tombstones are important in the culture of Darnley Island: their size and value are measures of the deceased's standing and esteem in the community. Their purchase is not undertaken lightly, nor are prices skimped. It was a singularly stupid white administration official who insisted a tombstone had to be obtained through approved departmental channels. Like the single shot that sets off a battle, that action set off George Mye into a life of island politics: 'I was hurt then, you know, and I said, You bugger. I'll get you one day, if it's the last bloody thing I do.'

Independence became his goal, independence from the control of the Queensland Government. He saw earlier than many the widening chasm of political direction between Queensland and the Commonwealth, and figured the ultimate power had to be where the money was. Increasing Federal Government interest in islander welfare was a key development. Mye found he was the sort of islander the Feds were looking for. Such people could prove wrong the Queensland approach to island affairs. Queensland was determined to continue a long-standing policy of paternal guidance of the island people. The Federal philosophy

FACES, PLACES ▲

was to find natural leaders and give them the chance to show what they could do, sink or swim. George Mye swam. He learned where the money bags were kept in Canberra and who had the keys.

Back he went to his island, with Canberra money for a Housing Co-operative, a faster boat for inter-island travel, and an assurance of reduced dependence on the State authority. And all achieved quietly, by playing the system. No demonstrations, no banners, no threats: just a natural-born systems man showing why his islands elect him to speak for them, and why no-one disputes George Mye is the smartest man on Darnley.

It Was All Right on the Night

The Playhouse is about the size of western Europe.

The cast live across the top end of the Northern Territory. In terms of European distance, the producer is in London, the players in the Hebrides off northern Scotland, and Bordeaux, Frankfurt and Copenhagen. They have no telephones, their only communication is through a scratchy and meteorologically unreliable radio system. Yet these people plan to produce a play, to recreate that celebrated Australian wedding rite which is as much social comment as entertainment, Jack Hibberd's *Dimboola*.

It is all in aid of School of the Air, Katherine School of the Air, which brings education to isolated children on stations, in camps and tiny settlements across the Top End. One of the mothers, Terry Underwood, has been south to one of the big cities and has seen the play. School of the Air needs money; the government funding is never enough, although the idea is an invention of the Australian outback and is internationally admired. Terry Underwood floats the idea across the air waves in the natter session, the open time for parents' conversation when school sessions finish, and the enthusiasm is immediate. It's never been done before, everyone's sure, and that's as good a reason as any to give it a go.

> *I saw a need to bring people together* [Terry Underwood said]. *We live in isolation geographically but I don't see why we should admit defeat. I thought we needed something to involve the fathers, and I thought people could relate to* Dimboola.
>
> *How can we raise funds for a school that's spread out all over the*

WAITING FOR THE WEDDING: THE CAST OF KATHERINE'S PRODUCTIONS OF 'DIMBOOLA' GOT TO THE THEATRE ANY WAY THEY COULD.

▲ A BIG COUNTRY

BELOW: *School of the Air, Katherine, NT.*
BERT WEIDEMANN/THE NORTHERN TERRITORY GOVERNMENT

OPPOSITE PAGE: *Downtown Katherine, and all the suburbs, too.*
BERT WEIDEMANN/THE NORTHERN TERRITORY GOVERNMENT

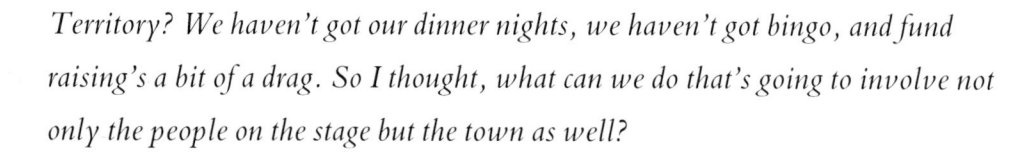

Territory? We haven't got our dinner nights, we haven't got bingo, and fund raising's a bit of a drag. So I thought, what can we do that's going to involve not only the people on the stage but the town as well?

Typically for an outback woman, Terry Underwood wasn't fazed by what the military would call the logistics problem she faced. The play eventually would be staged in Katherine, and the School of the Air there would have to be the focal point. But Terry, Producer and Actress, lived 600 kilometres away, and some of her cast were just as far out of town in the opposite direction—station owners and managers and wives, a pub keeper, a helicopter pilot. So they set up a drama time on the School of the Air network and, once school was out, the cast of *Dimboola* were in. For six months any Spy in the Sky snooping on the radio traffic of the Top End would have recorded a code-breaker's nightmare. (Imagine them, hunched over their computers at Langley, Virginia, or on Moskaya Prospekt, trying to crack the 'Katherine' code: 'Ar, put a cork in it Aggie. Why don't you two shut up. Oh geez, ain't this awful.')

The producer is out near the Western Australian border. The piano is in Katherine—fortunately, so is the pianist, so that's one break. The would-be actress 350 kilometres down the track has some lines to say, but when she opens her microphone she can't hear the music, so she can't get the timing.

As rehearsal follows rehearsal and people learn the words, the weather steps in. Summer is coming and with it a near constant barrage of static. At the best of times so far into the back country, radio communication can be hit and miss. To outside ears the signals the homestead speakers put out are an audio mess, a stream of distorted sound effects with snatches of voice broken in mid-word and

194

FACES, PLACES ▲

▲ A BIG COUNTRY

The radio room at Katherine: the teacher works one of the biggest schoolrooms in the world, the Northern Territory Top End.
BERT WEIDEMANN/THE NORTHERN TERRITORY GOVERNMENT

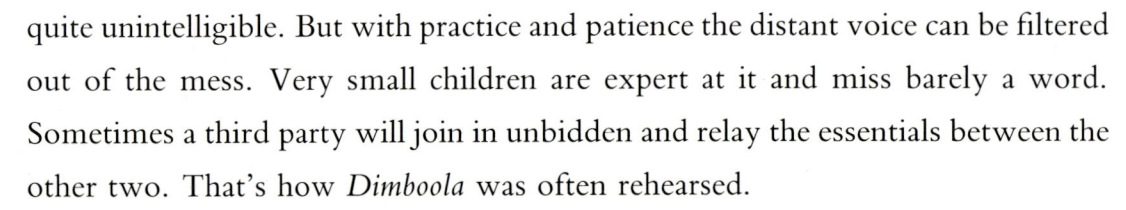

quite unintelligible. But with practice and patience the distant voice can be filtered out of the mess. Very small children are expert at it and miss barely a word. Sometimes a third party will join in unbidden and relay the essentials between the other two. That's how *Dimboola* was often rehearsed.

It's a pretty public network, anyone with a receiver can eavesdrop and, with no other entertainment on the air, the *Dimboola* rehearsals became an outback equivalent of radio soap opera. But there were many rehearsals and long before the play reached the Katherine stage there were people all over the Top End who could recite whole slabs of the dialogue, word-perfect. And they weren't even in the cast. Those who did have roles found themselves greeted by their *Dimboola* names instead of their own. The project took on a life of its own. But for all the enthusiasm, all the willingness, Producer Underwood found the radio just wasn't enough. She needed a rehearsal in the flesh. Could they, her scattered cast, make it to Katherine? Could they what?

Roz Lavercombe drove for fifteen hours to get there. It should have been only nine, but she kept doing tyres, five of them, and that was only one way. Her home was 900 kilometres from the footlights at Katherine, on the Gulf of Carpentaria. In they came, the whole cast: lines learned well enough, if not word-perfect, radio static edited out, some rough edges to round off, and a meeting to reassure each other that it would be all right on the night.

And of course it was. It was better than all right, it was a howling success. People used to improvising had done something that, as far as they knew, no-one had done before. Isolated people had found a sense of community. A theatrical impossibility had been achieved. The School of the Air had made some money.

And next, they thought, they might do *Macbeth*.

A Wedding in Katherine

Of course, the *Dimboola* wedding was all very well, but it was just pretend. There are still some people in Katherine who can remember a wedding that would have done any playwright proud, when Marie married Joe.

The wedding was a kind of Katherine town happening, a local property, the talk of the Territory for a while, and even the proposal had been a public event. Joe was carrying a crocodile at the time and he shouted his proposal, more in the nature of an ultimatum, across the road: 'You can marry me today or not at all,' he said. Ah! Romance!

'And so it suddenly hit me,' said the bride many years later, 'he meant it. It was the end of my run of playing him along, so I promptly said Yes. Half the township was gathered around sort of barracking at that stage. So, okay. The town promptly organised it, and we were married that night.'

That was the wedding of Marie and Joe Mahood: Marie, BA, journalist, city girl; and Joe, the one-time city boy who'd gone a-droving. Thirty years of outback life later, the Mahoods talked to *A Big Country*, on their Queensland brigalow property Cattle Camp, about events before and after the wedding that briefly livened up life in Katherine, Northern Territory.

But first, that crocodile that Joe brandished at the moment of his declaration of everlasting love and failing patience: it was long dead and had been amateurishly, and very badly, stuffed. Marie's sister had shot it and wanted Joe to take it back to Perth. The thing

Joe and Marie Mahood.

OPPOSITE PAGE: *JOE MAHOOD IN THE KITCHEN AT CATTLE CAMP. 'A DREAMER, AND A DOER.'*

was so obnoxious and odoriferous that Joe desperately wanted to be rid of it and was quite unconscious that he was using it to reinforce his proposal of marriage.

It was no sudden proposal. There had been an engagement of sorts for six months when Joe decided that was long enough and shouted his ultimatum across a wide street in Katherine, to have it accepted not just by Marie but by half the town as well.

Marie Mahood, thirty years on:

There was a hawker's van in town because of the races and they had one white dress. It wasn't my size, but one of the ladies in town cut it down to fit me. And lent us her wedding ring. There was a Salvation Army padre working as a carpenter for the Works Department, so they went around and saw him and, okay, after work tonight.

My sister's boss organised a wedding breakfast and Hessie, his wife, cut Joe's hair and Joe bought some long whites at the store and somebody pinched some roses from a garden, the only roses, because Katherine in those days was only two streets and two pubs. And everything was organised down to the wedding photos. A grader driver was in town and he had a film and some flash bulbs, and we had the lot.

A cake? I don't know who provided that. I was told later it was a couple of Big Sister cakes from the store. One of the women in town iced them, too. Tier cake, everything, and champagne and speeches, the lot organised in six or seven hours.

Which just about demolishes the old saw about marrying in haste...

After thirty years, four children and enough bush experience to fill the

FACES, PLACES ▲

▲ A BIG COUNTRY

OPPOSITE PAGE: GOOD LAND, THE BRIGALOW, AND CHEAP. BUT WHAT WAS IT GOING TO COST TO MAKE SOMETHING OF IT?

book and countless feature stories she's written, Marie Mahood says the interesting member of the partnership is Joe, 'a dreamer and a doer'.

It's not unusual to see a practical chap like Joe with the poetic touch, the romantic touch. Nearly everybody in the bush has these two sides, you know, the practical side when you've got to overcome the difficulties and the romantic side where you lie on your back on a swag and look up at the stars and think poetry.

I found when I first came into the bush that this artistic side that nearly everybody possessed was one of the things that made me feel that I identified more with the people in the bush than I did with people in the city. There seemed to be time to think about the artistic side, and to want, need, to put it down.

Marie and Joe are both putting it down, in their different ways. She writes, he paints, and at the time they spoke to *A Big Country*, Joe was being bold enough to think of selling up the place they call Cattle Camp and being a full-time painter. But, first, he'd need to finish what he'd started in Queensland's brigalow country, inland from Mackay.

The brigalow was opened for settlement in the 1960s and 1970s: good land and cheap, and terms that encouraged the battlers. It had the capacity to support big herds of beef cattle, but first it had to be cleared, fenced, improved. And the Mahoods, like others, under-guessed how much it was all going to cost. So they were years behind even their informal schedule. Marie was off the place a lot of the time, teaching in a mining town 100 kilometres away. That became necessary when the beef market crashed and they could barely give away animals they'd paid dearly for. But it came good, eventually, and the paper value of Cattle Camp doubled or even trebled. Marie went on teaching, 'to keep the tucker box filled'.

FACES, PLACES ▲

▲ *A BIG COUNTRY*

Joe and Marie—he paints, she writes. Both cherish the time to think about the artistic side of their lives.

And because, after a wedded lifetime of weekday separations and weekend reunions, that had become their way of life and it suited them.

'One long engagement,' Marie called their life, an engagement that hadn't really ended with that shouted exchange across the street in Katherine in 1952, and her decision it was time to stop 'playing him along'.

'I've Photographed a Million Women'

Time was when a string of coastal townships in southern Queensland had separate identities. There was Coolangatta, with its other half, Tweed Heads, a road's width and a State border away. Greenmount, Kirra, Surfers Paradise, Southport. It was all really one long, empty beach and it was inevitable it would become one long town. Gold Coast, they call it now, and the villages of old are locations within it, fashionable or otherwise, down market or up, high priced or less high priced. From the weekend break for Brisbane suburbanites, and the holiday resort for inland families, the place has become an Australian symbol for new money, quick profit and, seen across the water from down the coast a bit, the high rise looms like some misplaced Xanadu through the salt spray.

When Fred Lang first saw it, in 1935, he wouldn't have seen it at all until he was on top of it. The tallest building was a two-storey pub or a house on those unique Queensland stilts. Fred Lang? Who's Fred Lang? He was the Man in the Red Hat, the Beach Photographer, and by force of showmanship and personality, one of the first 'characters' the Gold Coast encouraged.

One morning, in the holiday season of 1935, Fred loaded his old camera and went to Greenmount beach to announce himself as the Beach Photographer. 'You're mad,' they had told him. 'You won't make a living here.' Before lunch on the first day, he had taken 400 photographs of people on the beach: families, children, shy young men, and the first of the million beach girls he would film in the next thirty years.

FRED LANG: AN EYE, AND A LENS, FOR BEAUTY.
FRED LANG

▲ *A BIG COUNTRY*

While others had their lunch, Fred was processing film and making prints. 'After lunch I went to the "studio" and there was a mob in front. I opened the door and they came in like a mob of wild buffaloes, nearly knocked the counter over. I sorted them out and everybody was happy, and from that day to this I haven't stopped working.'

Fred Lang wasn't a trained photographer. He wasn't a trained anything. He was a young man in tough times, inventive and self-reliant. Before discovering the pleasures of photographing on Queensland beaches, Fred had hawked door to door his own inventions. The Ace Fly Catcher was one, a tin can dispensing a honey-like substance along a trailing wire. One and threepence each, about twelve cents, and in some small towns Fred reckoned he'd sold one to every house. Then he went into patent medicines, mixing his own concoction of laxative and aspirin and selling it with the suggestion that whatever ailed the buyer, here was the cure in one product. Four pills for threepence. Cheap health care.

But all that ended with the discovery that people on holiday liked to be photographed, and would pay for it. When the boom began on the southern Queensland beaches in the 'fifties, Fred was there and established as the Beach Photographer. He wore a red hat to mark his presence and employed eighteen people to handle all the work. His best ever day: 1444 photographs. The total of his career: six million, he estimates. The most memorable: the English phenomenon Sabrina, a chesty blonde whose mammaries were very briefly among the wonders of the English-speaking world, and who enjoyed some notoriety in the colonies in the 'sixties. She accepted Fred the Photographer as her bodyguard and escort for a few days on the coast. And, of course, he photographed her. From one negative, Fred sold 10 000 prints. It was, he says, a high point of his life.

OPPOSITE PAGE: *Two in a million from Fred Lang's camera. The briefly famous Sabrina (left), his most successful shot ever.* FRED LANG
BELOW: *A cartoonist's view of Fred Lang.* WILSON COOPER

The Golden World

In the mythology of the gold rush, the townships that erupted on the diggings were tent and shanty towns, their streets of dust or mud and a business area where false-fronted buildings hid squalor behind presentable facades. But Charters Towers was different.

Charters Towers they called 'The World', and so rich were its mines they believed The World would last forever. Did it not have its own Stock Exchange, the very symbol of worth and permanence, and had not the rich, hard rock which underlay the town yielded treasure worth today four thousand million dollars? Of course it would last, and the buildings of Charters Towers were made to last accordingly.

By rights, the place would be called Charters Tors—tors meaning hills—but from the start of mining, newcomers had trouble with the old English word and Towers it became. The bright yellow metal turned up there in surface scratchings in 1871 and it was quickly apparent that this was no flash in the prospector's pan. This was big reef gold and, within a year, 4500 miners were working and a permanent town—a city by the standards of the time—was growing around the mines. Thirty batteries ground the rock down until it gave up its wealth: six and a half million ounces of gold came out of the Charters Towers mines before mining stopped in 1954, 183 tonnes of pure gold.

They built their town right on top of the lode. Six hundred metres under the main street the shafts and drives extend, and if it were possible to slice through the place, and study a section of it, an

Joe Donovan, gold miner.
OPPOSITE PAGE:
Traces of a golden past: old workings, Charters Towers.

FACES, PLACES ▲

▲ A BIG COUNTRY

BELOW: HARRY WEARE. 'GOLD MAKES THE DOLLAR LOOK SO PALTRY.'

OPPOSITE PAGE: TO SAVE ON COSTS, NORTH QUEENSLAND BUILDERS BUILT INSIDE OUT. THIS MINER'S COTTAGE AT CHARTERS TOWERS IS TYPICAL OF THE STYLE.

underground network would be revealed as complex as the inside of a termites' nest, deserted now, and flooded, but each shaft named and for a while famous, and each drive with its own record of riches: the Brilliant, two and a half million ounces (70 750 kilograms); the Daydawn, one and a half million (42 450 kilograms); the Queen, the Blackjack, the Imperial, the Ladybird, the One-And-All, the Just In Time.

But one by one, the reefs ran out and mining at The World dwindled and almost died. The big miners could no longer profit there, but there were some individuals who never gave up. They waited for The World to come to life again, as they knew it certainly would, and in the meantime they fossicked a living out of what was left. Because gold miners, real miners that is, not the burrowers-on-wages working for some multi-national excavator, but the old men who stay around mine sites when most people have gone, these men know the value of gold. To a man, they hold in contempt paper money, copper money, dubious nickel-and-God-knows-what alloy money. Gold is money, they believe, the only money. Gold is life, the reason for life, and the reward for life.

Said Henry Weare, holding a bar worth $10 000: 'It cheapens the dishonourable dollar. Makes it look so paltry.' But Henry was finding it hard to fossick enough gold to make a button, let alone a bar. There's still gold there, few in Charters Towers have any doubt about that, and a local legend says the richest untapped vein of all lies under the town centre, the park.

Joe Donovan had no doubts at all. He'd been working the old Ladybird for the best part of thirty years when, thirty-one metres down and forty metres along a western drive, he found the ore body that he knew just had to be there. Enough to make him a millionaire, he said with the sort of confidence that had

FACES, PLACES ▲

▲ *A BIG COUNTRY*

kept him digging without much mechanical help for half a lifetime.

Joe Donovan's find coincided with a new look at Charters Towers by some bigger operators. The gold price was on one of its journeys through the roof and the last mine on the field to close, the Blackjack, could maybe come to life again, not underground, at least for a while, but on the surface where lay the tailings, the mullock, the waste from three-quarters of a century of mining and milling.

They had brought to the surface from the mines of Charters Towers seven million tonnes of rock. The gold ran at about one ounce to the ton (thirty grams to the tonne), with the techniques for separation they had then. But techniques change and improve, and it's possible there's more gold in the mullock heaps of Charters Towers than was ever taken out. If the new methods of separation work economically, then The World could come to life again. But the action on the Stock Exchange will be far away, for that level of grandeur is unlikely to return.

OPPOSITE PAGE: *MINES SO RICH THAT MEN THOUGHT THEY'D LAST FOREVER: THE BRILLIANT AND ST GEORGE, CHARTERS TOWERS, PRODUCED 462,296 OUNCES OF GOLD—THAT'S NEARLY 14 TONNES—BUT WAS MINED OUT IN 22 YEARS.*
THIS PHOTOGRAPH IS PART OF THE SUNMAP PHOTOGRAPH COLLECTION

CROWN COPYRIGHT RESERVED

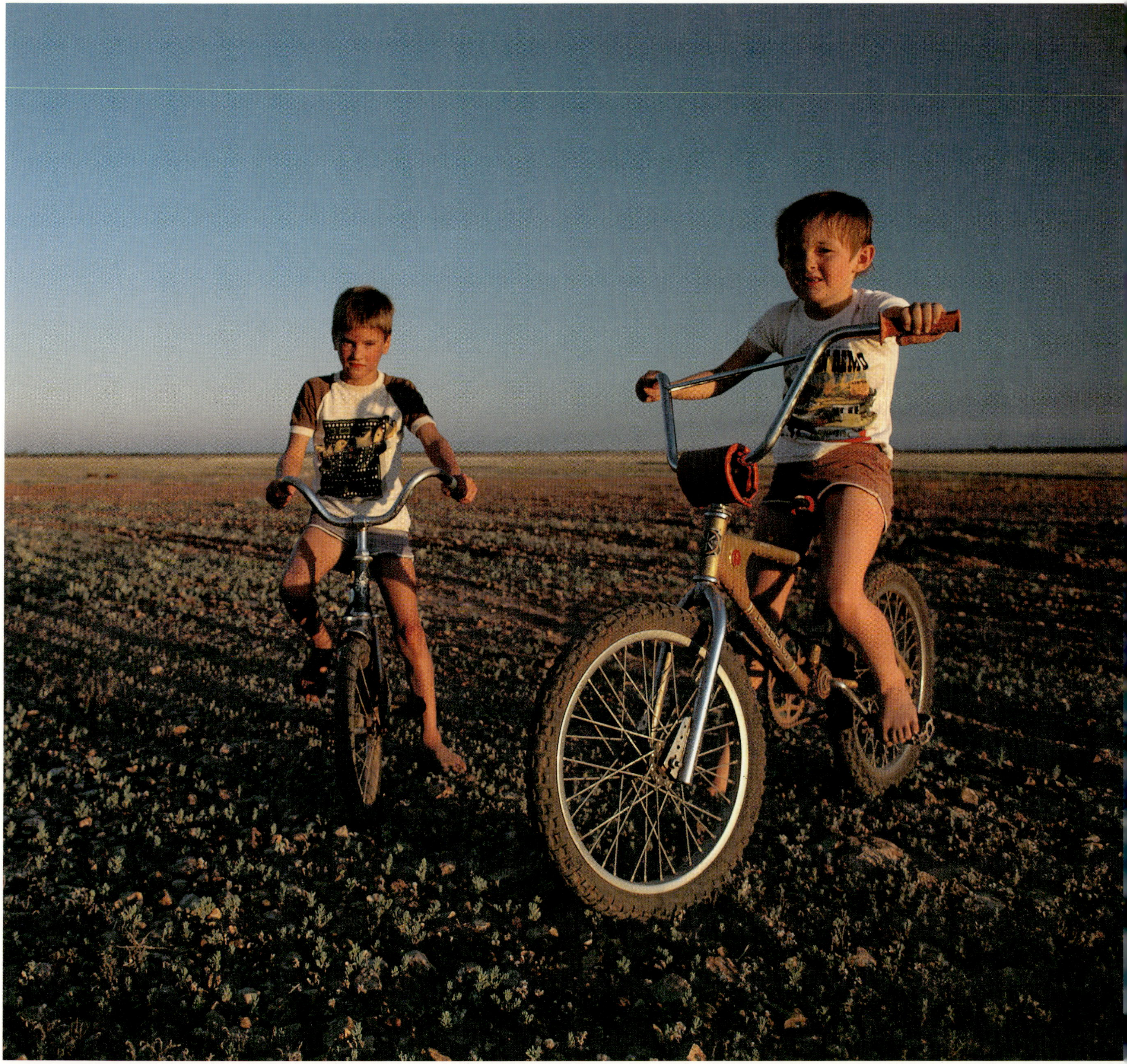

FAMILIES

WHILE URBAN AUSTRALIA *felt the accelerated process of change in the two decades of* A Big Country, *there remained places and people who felt change hardly at all. There was, and is, pioneering going on and often it's the kind of pioneering that opened up Australia more than a century ago. There are differences, of course, like machines. Transport and communications are better, but not everyone can afford the machinery, the light aeroplanes. The people who are still building outback Australia tend to be battlers, and they're still doing things in much the same way their great-grandfathers did. And, like their ancestors, they believe in big families. The statistical two-and-one-eighth-child families appear to prove that the statisticians don't often visit the outback where families like the Prices, all fifteen of them, are carving cattle runs out of wilderness.*

And far to the south, in Tasmania, A Big Country *found some old families whose elegant homes and elegant lives preserved an age that favoured the fortunate few.*

OPPOSITE PAGE: *Take away the river and the raft— Tom Sawyer and Huck Finn could have been Australian kids, left to make their own fun with whatever was available. A pair of BMX certainly help.*
COLIN BEARD/WELDON TRANNIES

All Right for Some

Best not to inquire too deeply how the grand Georgian houses of Tasmania were built. Cruelty built them, but time has washed off the stains of the barbarism of their building and now, in the Tasmanian Midlands, there's only the elegance to be seen.

There is a rare continuity of ownership here. In a country whose cities largely have been cobbled together out of ticky-tack since the mid-1940s, there's a craftsmanship and a quality peculiarly Tasmanian in these mansions of the Midlands, some of them built before the city of Melbourne was even Batman's village. They are fitted with the artefacts, the lamps, the silver of eighteenth century England, and furnished accordingly. They remain, many of them, in the ownership of direct descendants of the people who had them built. Ken von Bibra, of Beaufront:

> *When a person of considerable property arrived in Tasmania, he normally had a letter of introduction indicating his credentials, and from this, depending on the amount of capital he brought with him, he was given a grant of land commensurate with that amount of capital.*
>
> *In the Midlands of Tasmania there were three factors that brought about the building of these houses in the 1820s and 1830s—the golden era in Tasmania's history as far as Georgian homes were concerned. Firstly you had the availability of labour, in convict labour; secondly you had men of considerable capital who were prepared to build homes and houses such as they had been*

BEAUFRONT HOMESTEAD, TASMANIA.   ROBERT DREW

▲ A BIG COUNTRY

BEAUFRONT—THE GARDEN (TOP) AND SUNDIAL WITH THE STABLES IN THE BACKGROUND (BOTTOM).
ROBERT DREW

OPPOSITE PAGE:
BEAUFRONT HOMESTEAD, TASMANIA, FROM THE MAIN DRIVEWAY.
ROBIN MORRISON/READERS DIGEST
ROBERT DREW

accustomed to in England; and, thirdly, the stone that was found in the area was admirably suited to the Georgian style of architecture which these houses exemplify.

Ken von Bibra spent his childhood in the elegant homestead of Beaufront, and remembered it as a frightening place. To go upstairs, alone, at night on an errand for his parents was a scary expedition. He recalled climbing the stairs slowly, reluctantly, finding the book or glasses he'd been sent to get, then making a headlong dash back downstairs to the safety of company.

Beaufront is the centre of a property big by any standard, huge for Tasmania. Its 9308 hectares ran 28 000 sheep and produced more than 10 000 lambs a season. It employed fifteen men, called anywhere else stockmen but in Tasmania called shepherds. The house, the property, and the neighbouring houses and properties of the Midlands were caught in something of a time freeze. They were relics of a huge prosperity, traces of a time when, for the few, life was very grand indeed, and the owners appeared to have absorbed something of the character of the houses.

The world around them, however, was making problems for the lifestyle of old. For one thing, such houses were designed in the certainty of domestic servants being both available and affordable. Three parts through the twentieth century, they were neither.

The huge sheep runs which supported the grand houses were meeting the economic realities of changing times in farming. While the determination to preserve the houses and the lifestyle was there, practicalities dictated that parts of the houses be closed off and living space contracted to a manageable area.

It is possible that the Midlands families who welcomed *A Big Country* into

FAMILIES ▲

▲ *A BIG COUNTRY*

their historic houses will be the last generation to preserve them. By any economic measure, such houses are doomed, and while a sense of history may thrive better in such places and among such people as Midlands Tasmanians, the future for stately homes is almost certain to be decided, here as elsewhere, more by economics than by sentiment.

OPPOSITE PAGE: *BUILT IN AN AGE OF SERVANTS, THE GRAND HOMES NOW PRESENT PROBLEMS TO DO-IT-YOURSELF OWNERS.* ROBERT DREW

Henderson's Daughters

ABOVE:
THE HENDERSONS OF BULLO DOWNS.

OPPOSITE PAGE:
HENDERSON (TOP LEFT) AND
DAUGHTERS: MURRAY LEE (TOP RIGHT),
BONNY (BOTTOM LEFT) AND
DANIELLE (BOTTOM RIGHT).

In the Kimberley country of the western Northern Territory in the early 1980s, a story spread of three young women living on a remote cattle run, raised in near total isolation, working the station like men, speaking in soft American accents.

Many knew the story and wondered if it were fact or another of those outback legends. A few knew the place where the women were said to live, Bullo River Station, hundreds of kilometres from anywhere, a noisy and unreliable radio telephone its one tenuous link with the world. Fewer still had been to Bullo River and those few, very few, knew it was no legend. There were three young women with soft American accents living on Bullo River and working its cattle, welding its breakdowns, breaking its horses.

They were Henderson's Daughters, very real, very alive young women. The figure of legend was Henderson and the story of his daughters, told by *A Big Country*, was a story of a man whose thinking was out of tune with a world he found increasingly distasteful and who set out to replace it with one of his own.

Television showed Charles Henderson to be a tall, austere, unsmiling man. His words belied all that: his humour was as dry as fine wine, and quick. So quick that television missed a lot of it, television often needing a laughter and applause machine to tell us when a funny has occurred. Bullo Downs, he said, was the only female chauvinist operation in the Territory. It was a place of many chiefs, but it was hard to find the Indians.

Charles English Henderson III, of Virginia, United States of

220

FAMILIES ▲

▲ A BIG COUNTRY

OPPOSITE PAGE: *WOMEN'S WORK, BRANDING ON BULLO DOWNS.*

America, went to war when his country required it in the 1940s and flew aeroplanes off carriers in the Pacific. Honoured as an ace pilot, he surveyed the world in its new peace and found it not to his liking. The idea formed that he would make his own world. That's what brought him to Australia, that and the fact that he had married an Australian. Distance, he decided, would best protect his family from those elements of civilisation he disapproved of. That's what took him to the Northern Territory, to Bullo River, to the end of a fragile radio-phone link that served as a one-way window on the world.

Charles Henderson's views of what was good for his family drew on sources as diverse as the Jesuits, the United States Marines and the National Rifle Association. From the Jesuits and the Marines he took the philosophy that the tougher the treatment, the greater the strength developed by the treated. And he went out of his way to be 'a little bit hard on my family'. He wanted to protect his girls from what he saw as the malign influences of a society going more and more off the rails. Not for ever, but until they were old enough to cope. That's where the rifle parable came in: 'Well, it's like this. A rifle is more accurate than a pistol because it has a longer barrel. They've had a pretty fair barrel here so by the time they go into the outside world, they'll influence it, it won't influence them.'

The girls *A Big Country* showed living their station lives certainly were well prepared to influence the world. Murray Lee, the eldest, twenty-three at the time the film was made, had been in charge of the cattle on Bullo River since she was fifteen. Bonnay, two years younger, was the horse-breaker, fencer, welder and farm mechanic. Danielle, still recovering from the effects of boarding school 'outside', was learning the ropes of station life. She liked it: 'You're just so free out here. You feel closed in in the city; you've got to follow regulations, can't dis-

FAMILIES ▲

▲ *A BIG COUNTRY*

turb your neighbour. Your neighbour is five hundred miles [800 kilometres] away here. They don't care what you do. As long as you don't send any bushfires over the range they don't care. It's your life, you're allowed to do what you like.'

Not quite. The rule of Charles Henderson saw to that. Mrs Henderson, Sara, the Sydney girl Henderson chose to share his dream: 'He felt there was too much, and everything was too easy. He's a believer in discipline and character building, and he thinks adversity and challenge give this to a person.'

Murray Lee Henderson, Daughter No 1:

One reason he brought us out here is because he maintains that a person is a product of their environment, and he didn't like the environment outside. So he said, in my father's usual fashion, 'I'll make my own environment, Goddamn it.'

For years some people didn't even believe we existed because we just didn't ever leave here. We were always working so they used to stand off at a distance and say 'God, it's one of the Henderson girls. They've come out.' I'm not kidding. Some people are a little more standoffish also, because we do things that girls aren't supposed to do.

By which she means working cattle, riding shot gun in a helicopter at mustering time (that was another Henderson first in the Territory, using aeroplanes, and later helicopters, to muster his cattle. The neighbours couldn't believe it at first. Now, everybody's doing it), butchering, breaking, deftly wielding the knife that turns a potentially troublesome young bull into a potentially profitable young steer. These are the things girls aren't supposed to do, in the opinions of lesser men than Charlie Henderson. But then, rules like that weren't made for women like Henderson's Daughters.

OPPOSITE PAGE: *'GOD, IT'S ONE OF THE HENDERSON GIRLS.' MURRAY LEE, THE ELDEST OF HENDERSON'S DAUGHTERS.*

Survival of the Toughest

ABOVE: *Pat Tully*

OPPOSITE PAGE: *It's called the Channel Country, and the bird's-eye view shows why. The promise of wet season fertility brought the battlers of the eighteen hundreds.*

'Only the strong and the tough survived,' Pat Tully said of his ancestors. 'A lot of soft people came, but they died and they didn't pass their genes on. The people who couldn't have babies, who died when they had babies, the genes died with them.'

Darwinian evolution in action in Australia, a scientist might say, and it would be hard to dispute. The country Pat Tully talks about is the country where he has spent his life, the Channel Country in the far south-west of Queensland. It gets its name from the watercourses which dissect it. Cooper's Creek forms here from the coming together of two rivers, but the creek is not one stream, rather it is comprised of dozens of shallow channels which fan out across arid land on the fringe of the Simpson Desert.

Sometimes Queensland's tropical wet season will stretch far enough south and far enough west to bring heavy rains to the Channel Country. Then the channels flow and overflow and huge areas of land are under water. When the water recedes, it has brought to life the dormant native pastures and for a while there is lush feed for grazing stock. The promise of those good seasons brought the first settlers here. That, and the peculiar economic, social and political situations which applied in the more established areas of the colonies.

The pioneer families of the Channel Country had common histories intertwined for generations. They were Scots and Irish, mainly Irish, who had left the hunger and oppression of home and had come to Australia where there was gold to be found. They had found it, too, some of them, and what they had taken out of the

FAMILIES ▲

▲ A BIG COUNTRY

BELOW: *BUB KIDD OF MAYFIELD STATION.*

OPPOSITE PAGE: *MANY TIMES THE CHANNEL COUNTRY DENIES ITS PROMISE OF FERTILITY AND OFFERS ONLY HEARTBREAK. 'BUT YOU COULDN'T LEAVE,' SAID THE KIDD SISTERS, OWNERS OF MAYFIELD.*

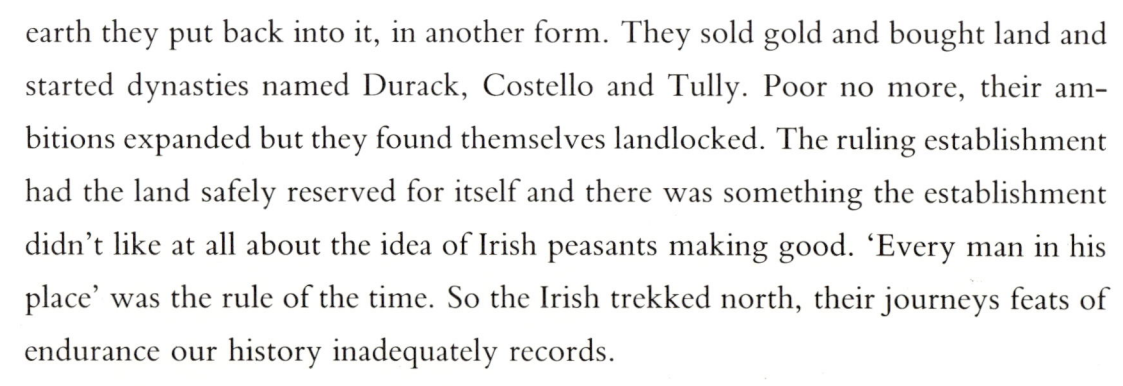

earth they put back into it, in another form. They sold gold and bought land and started dynasties named Durack, Costello and Tully. Poor no more, their ambitions expanded but they found themselves landlocked. The ruling establishment had the land safely reserved for itself and there was something the establishment didn't like at all about the idea of Irish peasants making good. 'Every man in his place' was the rule of the time. So the Irish trekked north, their journeys feats of endurance our history inadequately records.

The Duracks and Costellos were first; Pat Tully's grandparents, Patrick and Sarah, followed in 1874 and set up a vast run they called Toorachie.

They were intruders, invaders, and the country seemed to engage them in continuous guerrilla war. Drought besieged them. Storms would hit and run. Fire would strike when pastures were good and leave blackened ruin and hunger. And death would strike the weak and the unwary and the young, especially the young. Two, perhaps three of Sarah Tully's babies died, family records are inexact. Grandson Pat knows, though, that Sarah came to hate the Channel Country, and the hatred must have grown when one little tot wandered away while a visiting priest held Mass, and perished in the bush. Though the hard country had taken her children, Sarah Tully refused to yield them to it. She buried them temporarily and dug them up when she could and had the remains taken back south, to Goulburn, for proper burial.

But when Sarah died, no such noble gesture was possible and the Channel Country made its final claim on her. She's buried there, in the land she hated, and the home she and her descendants made, Toorachie, is dead too, its land absorbed by another station, its homestead abandoned and derelict.

It was once the social centre for an area bigger than Tasmania. 'We had a

FAMILIES ▲

▲ *A BIG COUNTRY*

FAMILIES ▲

marvellous time growing up,' Pat Tully recalls. 'We had the biggest parties you've ever seen, there'd be over a hundred people here.' He had gone back reluctantly to the old homestead: 'You don't enjoy looking at something that's dead.'

But over at Mayfield Station, things were being kept very much alive by the fourth generation of the Kidd family to run the place: there were three Kidd sisters and the youngest, called Bub, was seventy-five. The three had always had a hand in running Mayfield when their father and two brothers were alive, and as the only survivors the whole business relied on them. Kitty, the eldest, was still station book-keeper at eighty-two, and Meg, seventy-seven, was the gardener who could coax apples and oranges, roses and vegetables from the reluctant soil. Bub had always worked stock, for as long back as she could remember.

James Kidd had settled Mayfield around 1900. It was some of the best land in the Channel Country, and the Kidds lived in rare harmony with an Aboriginal tribe, the Buntamurras, whose children were the only playmates the three Kidd girls knew, and who taught them to live with the land, to fish and hunt and cook and eat goanna.

The Buntamurras are long gone; so are many of the families whose ancestors trekked in and settled the Channel Country. In the back of the minds of the Kidd sisters was the practical thought that the time was coming when they, too, would have to leave, forced off by the one onslaught of nature that all the courage and skill in the world couldn't beat: old age.

'Be nice sometimes to get away from the heat,' Kitty confessed, 'because as you get older, you can't face the conditions.'

But to leave? 'It would be like leaving your heart behind.'

OPPOSITE PAGE: ONCE THE SOCIAL CENTRE OF AN AREA THE SIZE OF TASMANIA, TIME HAS OVERTAKEN TOORACHIE HOMESTEAD, ABANDONED NOW AND QUIETLY DECAYING.
THIS PAGE, TOP: KITTY KIDD
BOTTOM: MEG KIDD

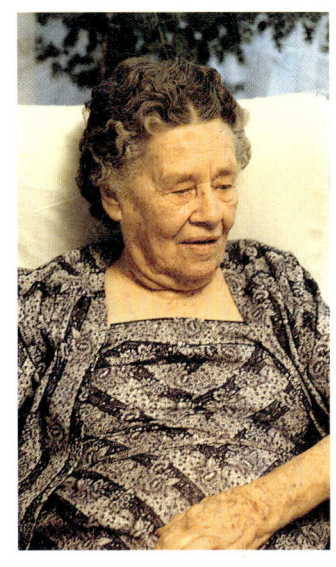

Pioneering the Present

THE PRICES, ALL 15 OF THEM.

OPPOSITE PAGE: *THE EDWARD RIVER, CAPE YORK.*
LEO MEIER/WELDON TRANNIES

Three parts of the way through the twentieth century, there was still pioneering to be done in Australia. But you had to go quite a way to find it. On the Edward River, on Cape York, on a vast station called Strathgordon, *A Big Country* found the Price family, twentieth century pioneers.

There were a lot of Prices—fifteen of them. Richie, head of the clan, had been a tobacco grower at Mareeba on the Atherton Tableland, with good towns nearby and plenty of neighbours on the relatively small and wealthy holdings. Tobacco gave him the financial backstop he needed to venture north, to the Cape, and into the cattle game.

Richie Price paid $120 000 for Strathgordon. Not a lot of money, but what he got for it was an area of land so big as to be almost incomprehensible to a tableland farmer: 5500 square kilometres of grassland and native forest. Thrown in were cattle, how many nobody knew, nor did anyone know where they were within twenty or thirty kilometres. They were animals that had returned to the wild and before they could be of any value to their new owners they not only had to be mustered, yarded, and hopefully, subdued, but actually found.

Richie asked locals how many cattle there might be on the run. The answer was that no-one knew and probably no-one would ever know, because most of the place had never even been explored, let alone mustered. In their first two years of ownership, the Prices had been over only half their land, but they'd seen enough to know

FAMILIES ▲

▲ A BIG COUNTRY

Richie Price, cattleman: years of rebuilding a run-down property.

opposite page: *Lights in the wilderness: in 5500 square kilometres, this night and every night the homestead at Strathgordon is the only light to be seen.*

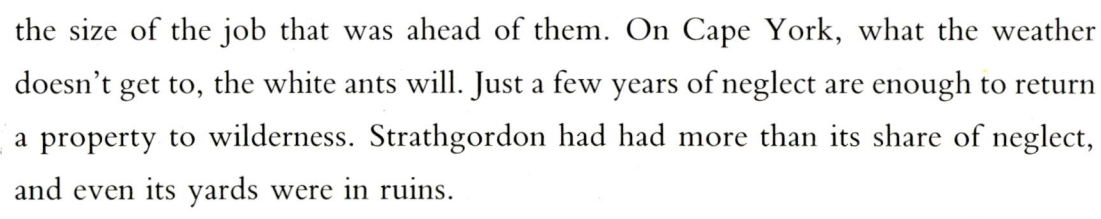

the size of the job that was ahead of them. On Cape York, what the weather doesn't get to, the white ants will. Just a few years of neglect are enough to return a property to wilderness. Strathgordon had had more than its share of neglect, and even its yards were in ruins.

Before he could even start looking for the cattle, Richie Price realised, and long before mustering, he would need yards to hold them. And not just ordinary yards, either, for he'd be fencing in animals that had never been yarded in their lives, and would be certain to jump or break out of yards that offered any weak point.

Into the bush, then, with axe and saw, to cut the 500 rails the first yard would need. In the far north of Queensland, there's no timber yard to ring when you need some wood, but all they need is on the property, and after six weeks' work the first yard is built. They're going to need twenty-three yards, at six weeks each: more than two and a half years of yard-building alone.

They had known it would be a lot of work; it was no surprise. What did catch Richie Price unawares was the extent of neglect Strathgordon had experienced, a neglect that aroused a quiet anger. 'Everybody that's been here has taken everything out and never put anything back into it again. Everybody's been taking and taking all the time, so we intend to put a lot of things into it. And we intend to stay here, not to take and move out.'

At the core of the Price family was Ruby May, married to Richie for a quarter of a century, mother of thirteen children, herself nearing fifty years of age and her youngest children only three and five.

She would cook an entire bullock every four of five weeks, wasting none of it. Eighteen loaves of bread a week, more if the stock horses got into the camp

234

FAMILIES ▲

▲ *A BIG COUNTRY*

and raided the bread bag. Right from the start of their marriage, Ruby and Richie decided they wanted to be self sufficient and the family was brought up thinking the same way. So they had little time in their lives for things outside Strathgordon, and that included schooling. One of the boys, sent to school in Cairns and initially doing well, began to pine so badly for home he lost weight at a dangerous rate and the school decided he'd be safer at home. So they brought him home and put him to work with his brothers, and he thrived. But for the parents, there was the nagging worry of an education lost.

All the children had left school early; the family was not one with a tradition of education. Ruby had little secondary schooling and Richie none at all. Despite the reasoning that if cattle prospered, all the children needed to know was how to run a station—and no school taught that—the Prices brought a governess to Strathgordon to teach some of the ways of the outside world. Not that the outside world and its ways are held in high esteem at Strathgordon: the Prices believed that there, on their five and a half thousand square kilometres, was just about all the world they needed.

The fifteen of them had a place in the world three-quarters the size of Denmark, bigger than Holland, two and a half times the American state of Connecticut. If cattle held up, its development would take the combined lifetimes of them all.

OPPOSITE PAGE: *RUBY MAY PRICE, THE HEART, THE CORE, THE MOTHER OF STRATHGORDON.*

Gulf Battlers

THE FORSHAWS OF YELDHAM.

OPPOSITE PAGE: *ENOUGH BREEZE TO JUST MOVE THE MILL. SOME DARKENING CLOUD AT DUSK. MAYBE SOME RAIN OVERNIGHT? WE COULD DO WITH IT.*
DENSEY CLYNE/MANTIS WILDLIFE

Far to the south-west of Strathgordon *A Big Country* found another station, Yeldham, also owned and worked by a tight family group, the Forshaws, and the Forshaws, too, were pioneers. But they were doing it the harder way, with no outside income source to carry the first difficult years. The Forshaws were people battling to break even as a first step towards getting ahead, and the program accurately called them the Gulf Battlers.

Elton Forshaw had been a stockman all his forty-odd years. He'd got to be head stockman, then manager, on Riversley. Maude was the station cook. After a dozen years of running someone else's business, Elton wanted something of his own. He had no money and there wasn't much property around at that price. But there was Yeldham. Close to Riversley, as distances run in the Gulf, it was familiar country with known problems and known strengths and small by Gulf standards, only about 520 square kilometres. And there was one huge advantage: it was cheap. The Forshaws became station owners for 25 000 borrowed dollars and drove onto their place in an old station wagon, a caravan and a battered Land Rover, carrying together everything they owned. They had four saddles but only one horse, the gift of a friend. They had no stock and no money to buy any. To break that vicious circle, Elton and his older son, Les, went working for others, as fencing contractors, and, at Yeldham, twelve-year-old Ian found himself the man of the station.

They were hard years, Leslie Forshaw remembered. He was fifteen at the time. They worked four or five years fencing on Lawn

FAMILIES ▲

▲ A BIG COUNTRY

OPPOSITE PAGE, LEFT: *ELTON FORSHAW, STOCKMAN. HEAD STOCKMAN. THEN MANAGER. NOW STATION OWNER. NOT BAD IN 40 YEARS.*
RIGHT: *IF THE BUSH LIFE HAS ITS PLEASURES THAT THE TOWNSFOLK NEVER KNOW, FEW OF THEM COME THE WAY OF THE COOK. THE KITCHEN, YELDHAM STATION, IN QUEENSLAND'S GULF COUNTRY.*

Hill, dawn till dark, seven days a week. 'Maybe a bloke's mad,' Les said, explaining his decision to stay in the fencing business as a contractor. He regretted his lack of schooling, another two or three years would have made a difference and he sometimes felt disadvantaged. What lessons he had came from Maude, his mother, because the Gulf Country is light on schools and governesses were far beyond the finances of the Forshaws.

The older Forshaw daughter, Valmae, was seven when her father and brother went fencing to raise capital, and she started early to earn her keep, minding the family's little flock of goats. Her sister Joanne was goatherding from age five. The man of the place, Ian, left at fourteen to join his father and brother on the fencing contracts and Yeldham had to be run by Maude and two young girls. The men came home in emergencies, but fences were fixed, bores maintained, by the women.

It took Elton seven years to earn the capital his station needed. He and the boys would work in the Dry and come home in the Wet to do what work was possible around the place during the monsoon season. All the available money went on stocking and necessities, there was nothing left for personal comfort. The only weatherproof buildings were caravans; these the family used as bedrooms. The house building was unlined and lacked even doors. It leaked, and to drown out the drumming of the monsoon rain and the maddening rattle of the frogs, they turned up the volume on the battery powered cassette player and let Slim Dusty reassure them there was a world outside the Gulf Country.

Ten years into their struggle to make something of Yeldham, the Forshaws were still far from prosperous, but they had broken the bonds of deprivation and could see at least the hope of the future they had sought when they convinced a

FAMILIES ▲

▲ *A BIG COUNTRY*

helpful bank manager Yeldham could be made to pay its way. They were out of debt, at last. Elton was a Councillor on Burke Shire, putting something back, he said, into the country that was giving him his chance. There was talk of building a proper house, but it was Maude who said it might be better to wait a while and put the building money into a new bull or two to improve the herd. Comfort, success, prosperity, the new house, would all depend on the cattle and the beef price staying up. If it didn't, 'We'll probably patch up our little shed again,' said the Gulf Battler.

OPPOSITE PAGE: *SUNSET IN QUEENSLAND'S GULF COUNTRY.*

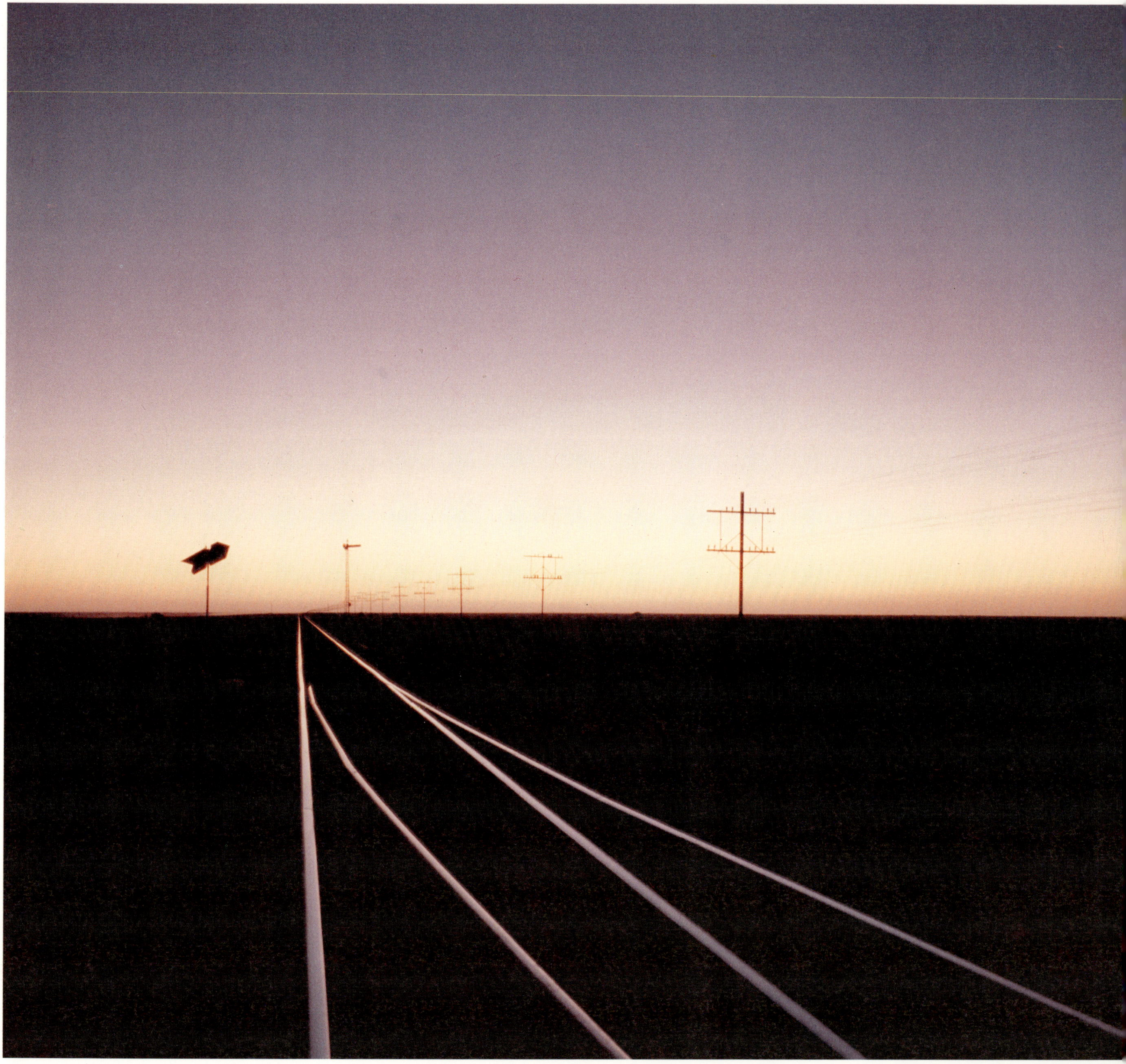

TRENDS

TWENTY YEARS is a time span long enough for a trend to become first discernible, then established, then a part of life and no longer a trend.

The twenty years of A Big Country began as the first computers were becoming established in Australian business and government, the first containers were promising a shipping revolution, the new rural class called the Hobby Farmers were meeting a mixed reception as city money met country tradition, and men and machines were meeting in competition for rural work. In the sugar fields, and in most other rural industries, the machines were winning and the remaining gangs of canecutters were being paid off.

Canecutters displaced by machines, clerks uprooted by computers, people looking for life after the death of the cities and people looking for some meaning and satisfaction from work, found in the relative prosperity of the seventies a chance to do something different, so an ex-canecutter who had been careful with his dollars could buy a small farm, three ex-shearers could experiment with the hand-making of furniture, and the hobby farmer, on his place in the country, could learn an inland version of what weekend sailors had long known about their hobby: it cost!

OPPOSITE PAGE: *Tracks across the Nullarbor Plain.* KATHIE ATKINSON

Standing in a Dust Storm Tearing Up Money

Two decades on from the start of *A Big Country*, the words Hobby Farming have an altogether different meaning, and arouse different reactions, from the time the program first remarked on a reversal that was occurring in the long-established drift of Australians away from the land. People were drifting back to the land, city people, prosperous people, fed-up people. Someone had invented a new word, Lifestyle, and these new migrants wanted their share of it. It existed, they thought (perhaps their race memories told them), in the bush.

It is a phenomenon of such social strength that *A Big Country* has returned to it more frequently than any other subject. The program tries to avoid re-visits, and gains from that determination. There is an industry joke that some places, some issues, some points of crisis are so beloved by television that a cameraman, visiting for the first time, need only look for the tripod marks on the ground to know where the best shots are. But it's also possible to leave people and issues up in the air after a half-hour's examination. There are seldom answers to the later question, 'I wonder what happened to...?'.

A Big Country discovered the new drift back to the bush early on; not that they had to search far and wide, because an hour and a bit's drive from the program's Sydney office was a district the hobby farmers had made their own. It's called the hills—foothills would be more accurate, where the land folds gently at first then more sharply from the coastal plain into the Blue Mountains.

FOLLOWING THE HORSES: A NEW MEANING FOR THE FAWKNER FAMILY.

▲ A BIG COUNTRY

OPPOSITE PAGE: *A Place in the Country, Australian style. But at what price?*

It was where Australian agriculture began: a century before, just about every orange eaten in Australia was grown in the hills. Then came the egg farmers, the market gardeners and, finally, the city's prosperous, waving their cheque books generously and offering for a few hectares a kind of money the owners knew they'd never make from honest toil. The subdividers came too—sharks, some of them, venturing unusually far inland from the coast. The collapse of the citrus industry was a happy coincidence for some. It put on the market land treasured by families since the original convict grants were made, and the prices the developers were offering saved some people from ruin.

The subdivisions spread. Land close to the cities became extremely valuable, beyond the means of the majority of seekers after the good life who had to look further afield, to land around country towns, where the subdividers had bought up small farms, made them even smaller and sold them at huge profit. Some of the worst farmland in Australia found a market like this, but some of the best, too, and established communities were divided in their approach to the newcomers.

There was resentment, the feeling that land which had felt the sweat of three generations of farmers had become nothing more than a playground, that soil would be ruined, animals neglected, by the weekend farmers who swept in Friday night in their four-wheel-drives and played at country life for a couple of days. There was a component of jealousy, too, because the newcomers were so often so obviously prosperous.

The change in attitude began in country businesses. Proprietors found their takings increasing, their sales rising, their prosperity better than it had been for years. The newcomers were spending, spending on the land, the fences, on

TRENDS ▲

▲ A BIG COUNTRY

OPPOSITE PAGE: *This is not the excavation for a swimming pool, but the result of long-term neglect of the land. To put right erosion damage like this needs either national will or hobby farmer money. The national will seems lacking.*

houses, machinery. The bush was getting an enormous injection of unexpected city money. The weekend farmers were themselves a new primary industry and their greatest strength was that theirs was a labour of love: they were in the bush because they wanted to be, not because lives and times had trapped them there, and the ones who were serious about it found that once-closed communities were opening up for them.

They found the simple life was not the easy life; work was never ending. Nor was it cheap. Ownership of that place in the country could be like owning a boat, and the boat-owner's lament about cold showers and cost could be translated to the hobby farmer's experience, 'like standing in a dust storm, tearing up money', because the move to the bush was a bonanza not only for land developers and salesmen: Government and Local Government were in there, too, with hands outstretched for fees and taxes and rates. The dream of rural self-sufficiency on a small holding proved elusive for a majority. The reality for most was a struggle for financial survival. The country towns couldn't provide jobs for their own people, let alone the newcomers, though an occasional opportunity was there for men or women with special skills.

Geoff Fawkner, who took his young family bush in Victoria, found there was 'a very fine line between rural charm and rural squalor'. In the *Big Country* program called 'Jumping Off', Geoff and Aileen Fawkner told the story of a bush venture that had all the odds against it.

A public servant, living in Melbourne's Fitzroy, Geoff sought life beyond the public service. They sold up in the city and bought ten run-down hectares near Maryborough, land chewed at by diggers in the Victorian gold rush and later stripped of its fertility by generations of poor farming. The Fawkners wanted the

TRENDS ▲

▲ *A BIG COUNTRY*

simple life. But perhaps not quite as simple as it turned out: two-and-a-half years of living in a makeshift, dirt-floored hut; no electricity; no running water. They used the time to build a mud brick house, sun-powered as far as possible, but still a long way from completion.

Geoff Fawkner: 'It's interesting to see the difference between the reality of living an alternative lifestyle to what you imagined before you came or what's portrayed in the press or by those armchair grass-rooters who want an image of golden sunshine over the paddocks and faithful Dobbin plodding away.'

For the Fawkners, reality was the timeless hostility of bush Australia. Nature visited on them two of the black horsemen of the bush, drought first, then fire. Drought, and no money for hand feeding, meant they couldn't keep all their flock of goats, the planned income earner. There was precious little money for family feeding either, and the goats were eaten. There was a lot of curried goat that year, Geoff said.

Drought prepared the way for fire, the destroyer. The sheds went, the vegetable garden, fruit trees and all the fences. It was very nearly the end of everything. Aileen found a clerk's job in town and Geoff found a new reality of life in the bush: domestic duties, the washing, the cooking, the looking after kids. Not that he minded, but it got in the way of the things that needed doing around the place, the things he'd rather be doing than keeping the fire in the stove alight and doing the washing by hand. He learned what was meant by labour-saving appliances, because he didn't have any.

'It's a long step to cook something. You've got to cut the firewood, you have to bring it in, you have to chop it up, put it in the stove, keep an eye on the stove...'

OPPOSITE PAGE: *LIFE AND DEATH IN A FARM DAM: SURFACE RIPPLES SOFTEN AND DISTORT THE AFTERMATH OF BUSHFIRE.*

▲ A BIG COUNTRY

In the words attributed to a politician of the time, Life Wasn't Meant To Be Easy. The Fawkners weren't looking for an easy life, which was just as well, because their life in the bush was infinitely more complex and difficult than was suburban existence in Fitzroy. But it was what they wanted. 'Life's just a short instant,' Geoff said. 'If you're not happy in work or career or lifestyle then you should change it. You should do what suits you and be willing to take the risk. Y'know, jump off.'

Hydrogen, Carbon and Sweat

There's a polished television commercial about sugar, the industry's answer to fashion, fad and health fears. They're welcome to the argument, both sides, but the images of the advertisment are redolent of the Big Country where the tall, sweet grass grows, and where for so long it was the symbol of prosperity. The prosperity came at a price, however. Hydrogen and carbon are the principal components of sugar, but to make it in the old days another element was necessary. It was sweat, and it soaked the cane fields, the railways, the mills and the wharves of the sugar coast from the time the industry began until the machines came and men sweated no more.

The change came with a suddenness that caught a lot of people unaware, but from the time the canecutting machine was invented it was clear to all except the diehards that the blackened, sweating men with the machete-styled cane knives had little future left. Late in the age of the canecutter, *A Big Country* found Wes Johnson and his gang of cutters working their last season on the Clarence River in the north of New South Wales, where sugarcane-growing began in Australia, where the first canecutters had worked, and where the last would be pushed aside by machines.

Sugar had brought a kind of slavery to Australia—the infamous Kanaka trade from the Pacific Islands came out of the early belief that canecutting was not work for white men. When the unions decided that it was, after all, work fit for the gods of creation, the canecutter became a national legend.

He deserved the fame, as he deserved the big money the

WES JOHNSON CUTTING CANE.

▲ A BIG COUNTRY

OPPOSITE PAGE: *CANE FIRE, QUEENSLAND. THE THEORY WAS THAT FIRE DISPOSED OF THE VERMIN LIKE RATS AND SNAKES AS WELL AS THE UNDERGROWTH. IT MADE A DREADFUL MESS OF WASHING AND CURTAINS IN NEARBY TOWNS, TOO.*
DENSEY CLYNE/MANTIS WILDLIFE

legends said he was paid, for there wasn't much else in his working life. There was a job for less than half the year: eight hours a day spent doubled over, aiming the swinging knife accurately at the stalk just millimetres above the soil, covered in the first five minutes of the day in the black ash from the fire set the night before in the pious hope of driving out the unwanted biting and crawling and disease-bearing creatures who lived in the ripening cane.

There were nights at the pub, in little towns which offered nothing more than booze in the way of social amenities and, for the itinerants, a bed in the basic barracks the cane farms provided. And in the morning, sharpen up the knife, blacken up the body, slash into the cane and sweat the beer of the night before back into the rich red soil. Don't worry about the snakes, they'll keep out of the way and the noise, but worry, quietly, about what you can't see but you know might be there: the bugs, the germs, of the awful Wehl's disease, spread by the urine of rats. Fatal, and only too easy to get through a break in the skin.

Hydrogen, Carbon and Sweat. Sweat from the fireman stoking up the furnace on the little locomotives that hauled the cane to the mill. Sweat in the mill, in the heat of furnaces that made the steam that drove the machines that crushed the cane that made the sugar that used to go in bags to the wharves. Sweat on the wharves, where a ship-loading system, unchanged since the Phoenicians, dropped bagged sugar into the holds of ships that used to take a month to load. Then, when some overseas markets wanted bulk sugar, the bags were slit, manually, and the stuff tipped into the holds by sweating wharfies.

That's how it had been from the start of the industry, when *A Big Country* found Wes Johnson, a master of his dying trade. Five in his gang, and they boasted they could cut more cane in a day than any other gang on the Clarence River. And

TRENDS ▲

so they could. But on a nearby farm, the future was working: a machine was cutting 400 tonnes a day and even the best gang on the Clarence could manage only an eighth as much.

Wes was Ganger, the leader rather than the boss, and acknowledged as the gun cutter of the five. For the job had an endless competitive edge to it, each man trying to show he was better, faster. No reason, other than pride. The gang had a quota to cut, around twenty-five tonnes a day, and each man would share equally in the pay. Honour demanded you do your share; pride dictated you tried to do a bit more than that. Canecutting shared with shearing this silent effort to be better. Two of the hardest jobs men have ever been paid to do produced a work ethic that had never gone with the times into manufacturing industry or services or transport or clerking.

'Wes is a good ganger,' Neville Condrey said. 'He understands men and he can control them. He understands cane, and what it's worth. He's a good leader. Ganger's got a really thankless job because he's got to satisfy his men, he's got to please the farmer and the mill, the cane growers and all...' The admiration was mutual. Johnson considered Condrey the best canecutter he'd ever seen.

'You've got to have a hungry ganger,' said Wes Johnson. 'If you've got a hungry ganger you make money. Payday, the gang love him.'

As well they might, because the ganger was the middleman between the gang and the ultimate boss, the man paying the wages. If a crop were down, from wind or rain, the cutters could demand more money. If the stalks were too small, the rate went up. If it were sticky, wet, damp or too dry, the ganger would negotiate a special rate with the grower. That rate would depend on the negotiating skills of the ganger. He was time-keeper, and would decide where the burn-off fires should be lit. For all this, the ganger earned an extra one dollar a day.

Wes Johnson had taken his gang through the cane fields of North Queensland, working down the coast as the crops ripened, but the time had already come when there was no work for canecutters in North Queensland. The local invention of the mechanical cutter, a world first for Australia, was inevitable because good manual cutters just weren't available. Each year, the legendary 'sign-ons' at Canegrowers' Halls in the sugar towns saw fewer and fewer men offering for work, and the growers needed to be sure they could get their crops harvested when their sugar content was at its peak.

Gerald Egglington, a cane farmer on the Clarence River, mourned what he called 'The Men of Yesterday', but he knew why the next generation didn't want to fill their blackened, knife-scarred boots: 'It's understandable,' he said, 'when we have men on the moon and flying round the world in satellites and we're asking people to come out and sweat and toil like the old canecutter used to.'

A few stayed on to the very end, and they cut that last man-cut crop on the Clarence. Wes Johnson had seen more than one old-timer throw his knife into a canefield and say 'That's It. That's the Finish' at the end of the season, only to front up again at the next sign-on. Why? It was a way of life, and it's nice to live a legend, especially when you were best. That's the memory Neville Condrey took with him when he threw down the knife. He'd been one of the best, but he didn't let his skill, his reputation, his pride blind him to the inevitable: he knew he was one of a dying race, and he'd bought some land for his future.

No-one then ever dreamed that this rich industry itself faced hard times, that markets would collapse, and some cane farmers, left with the investments and the debts, might envy the cutters who'd got out when the going was good.

You Can't Carve the Silence

THE WORKSHOP, PORT LINCOLN, SA.

OPPOSITE PAGE: *BERNIE KOKER, MASTER CRAFTSMAN, PRESERVING THE BALANCE OF THE BUSH IN FURNITURE INTENDED TO LAST FOR GENERATIONS.*
ROBERT HAARBURGER

'You can't actually carve the gum trees with all of their leaves,' said Ken Martin, the wood carver. 'I don't think you can compete with nature at all. The first thing I appreciate about the bush is the silence and, of course, you can't carve silence.'

Ken Martin, Malcolm Averill and Bernie Koker are modern-day craftsmen, working in wood to make articles of use and beauty that may outlast their makers by centuries, as the woodworking triumphs of the past are the revered and highly valued antiques of today. Their work is different, and not only because of the timbers they use, the timbers of Australia; they try to design and make according to the same principles that guided the classic woodworkers of Europe, to conform to the shapes and proportions of nature. That meant measuring the bush, relating tree to tree and branch to branch, studying the numbers in search of constants, or patterns. They believe they've found the pattern, the shape of the Australian bush, and they seek to maintain it in the shapes and proportions of the furniture they make.

These three came not out of trade school or crafts class, but out of the shearing shed. Chance meetings brought the realisation that each expected more from life than the removal of the maximum amount of wool in the minimum length of time. They were shearers, Bernie Koker said, just to earn money: 'None of us had found any appeal in any of the alternative lifestyles that were presented to us, because we were basically activists and it dawned on us that perhaps it was possible for us to create a situation or a place

TRENDS ▲

▲ A BIG COUNTRY

Wood inlays from Bernie Koker's craftmanship. His reputation now is such that people wait months for made-to-order pieces, and his work appears in Canberra's new Parliament House.
ROBERT HAARBURGER

where three of us could work together and form perhaps a new ideology that would suit us in terms of our concepts of life.'

What all three wanted was to make things of quality, to pursue craftsmanship, to achieve a situation in which work was no longer just work, but a way of life. With a combined capital of just eighty dollars they opened a workshop in Port Lincoln, South Australia, and waited for seekers after quality to find them.

The paucity of capital belies the thoroughness of their preparations. Malcolm Averill had worked with his craftsman grandfather for two years, then joined a craft firm in England until they 'went plastic'. Ken Martin was a bushman, with a natural love for woodwork, and Bernie Koker's studies had traced furniture making back to the sixteenth century. Their search for perfection in design and execution led down some odd byways, into Greek philosophy, for instance, hardly the stuff of the woodworking shop, but the source of the look of 'rightness' so characteristic of classic design.

The Greeks, they found, had measured the European countryside in a search for perfect proportion, and had discovered a mathematical way to define natural proportion. Translated to measurements, the Port Lincoln trio believed, that discovery was the explanation of the timeless rightness of buildings, furniture and artefacts produced by the craftsmen of the classic age. Could they, in twentieth century Australia, define mathematically the Australian environment and reproduce it in items that would be classics of this age?

'We set about measuring,' Bernie Koker said, 'not quite knowing what to expect, but just measuring: the approximate height of trees; the girth at the bottom; the approximate leaves to a branch. We discovered that certain numbers did begin to reappear. There was something here that represented the same continuum, the same proportionalism, that existed in the European analogy.'

Measurements found, the search began for materials. The three had come late to woodworking in Australia, too late for ready access to the superb timbers that once grew here but had been squandered in the early lust for ring-barking, clearing and burning. They knew the stories, of course, of cedar used in fence posts and shearing sheds, jarrah exported to carry the rails of the London underground, and the more modern scandal of mature hardwoods ground into chips to make cardboard boxes to contain the Japanese export drive.

The search for what was left took them to unexpected places and brought to their notice the merits of unexpected woods. A casuarina yielded wood to make a desk, wood as good, Bernie Koker said, as the prized Honduras mahogany. In a Melbourne garden, a tree surgeon found a European oak that was past help and it wound up in the Port Lincoln workshop. The partners found some South Australian blackwood, a real rarity, and some Queensland walnut.

Did it concern them, to be using timbers that faced extinction? Not at all, because they weren't using up the timber, destroying it, grinding it into chips or burying it under fences or railway lines. They were making from it works of craftsmanship which, hopefully, would be treasured long beyond the life of the trees from which the wood had come. Bernie Koker believed that furniture was the only way some species would be remembered, all living examples having gone. He and his colleagues were making pieces for use three and four generations on. That would be one measure of their success. Another would be the training of apprentices, the passing on not only of skills but of values and beliefs about the precious place of craftsmanship in the lives of the few people who regarded it not as work, but as a way of life.

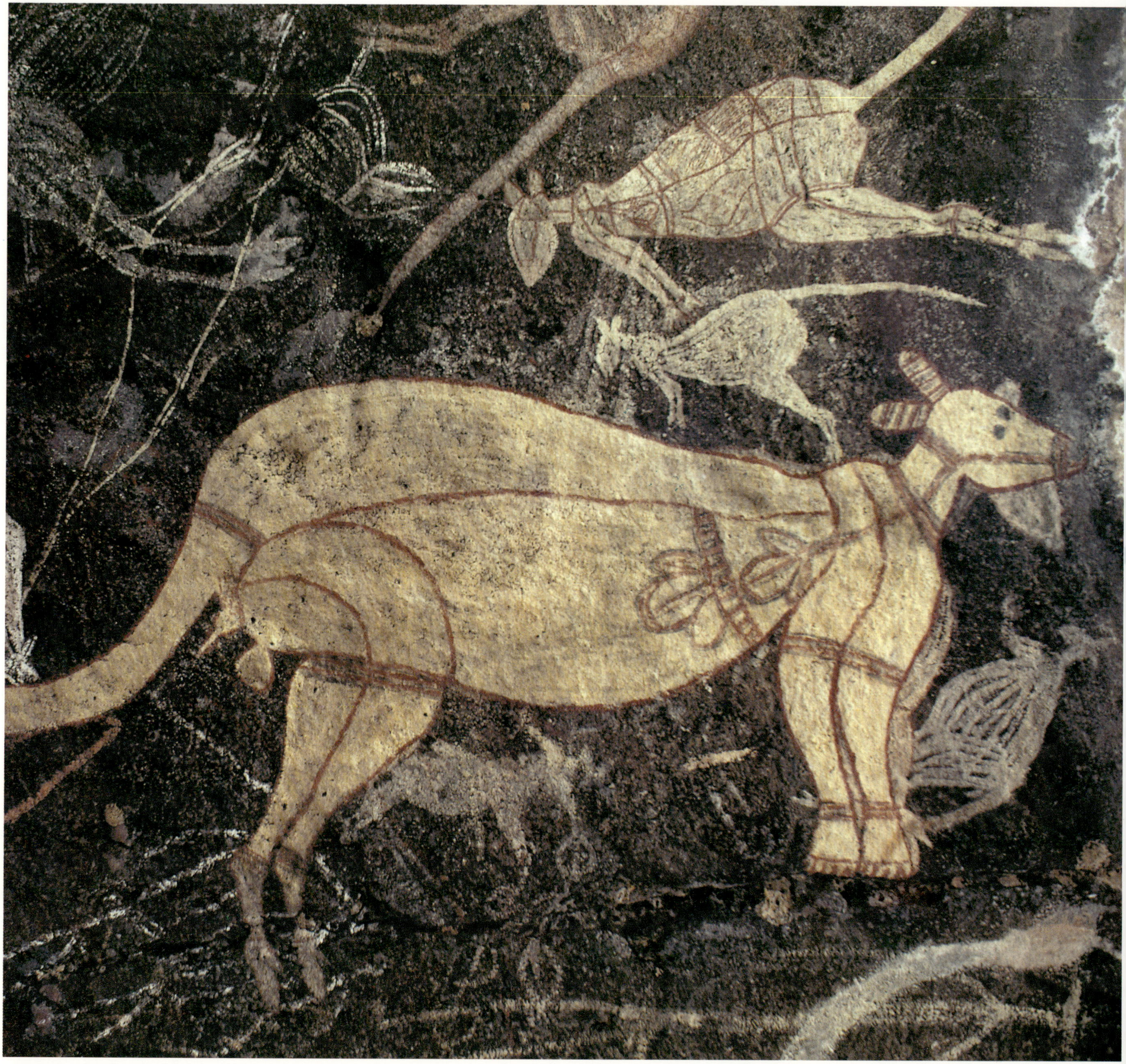

An Accounting

BALANCE SHEETS *were never the business of* A Big Country. *Inevitably, though, from the torrent of talent that flowed through the program there would emerge sometimes people whose ideas would demand debate, whose insights would challenge traditional beliefs, whose analyses of where we'd come from and where we might be going called for a kind of national balance sheet.*

The balance was often found to be in the red, our withdrawals from the Big Country had exceeded our deposits. The two hundredth anniversary of the opening of the white man's account gave two historians, one an outback amateur, the other an academic professional, cause to call for statements of account, and to warn that some repayment was overdue.

OPPOSITE PAGE: *Aboriginal rock art, Christmas Caves, NT.*
JEAN-PAUL FERRERO/AUSCAPE INTERNATIONAL

To Measure the Past, Use the Right Clock

Geoffrey Blainey looks askance at Australia's national birthday party. Two hundred years, two thousand, twenty thousand? In measuring the age of our country, Blainey says, we've used the wrong clock.

Perhaps we'd do well to listen to the man. He is one of our leading historians, and he, better than most, knows the traceable history of Australian man extends over not two hundred years but somewhere much closer to fifty thousand. It was that long ago that a human being drew on the wall of a cave a picture of one of his kind catching a kangaroo by the tail. That is the oldest trace of man in Australia.

Primeval boat people settled Australia, Professor Blainey says, people who were the most successful seafarers up to that time.

We don't know the year, we don't even know the millennium. Whether it was winter or summer we have no idea. But whatever the day those first Aboriginals waded ashore, that was Australia Day. Not 1788, but that remote day when the Aboriginals discovered this land.

The British settlers came to Australia with their family clocks, and in their kitchens and drawing rooms they put up the clocks and heard them ticking away at the beginning of Australian history. They thought Australian history began in 1788.

On present evidence, the Aboriginals have been here some 50 000 years. If we look at one of those old settler clocks, then the

'NATIVES OF NEW HOLLAND'. FROM PARKINSON'S JOURNAL, ONE OF THE EARLIEST IMPRESSIONS OF AUSTRALIANS.
STATE LIBRARY OF NSW

▲ A BIG COUNTRY

OPPOSITE PAGE: *THE ABORIGINALS: THEIR LIVES OFFERED A FREEDOM NOW VANISHED FROM THE EARTH, AND A PLENTY RARE IN HUMAN HISTORY.*
WELDON TRANNIES

Aboriginal history runs for more than fifty-nine minutes of the hour, in fact for fifty-nine and three-quarter minutes, leaving our history since 1788 to cover the last quarter minute. What we've seen since Governor Phillip arrived is the tail end of our history.

The 'natives' the first European settlers encountered were dismissed as primitives because in no respect did they measure up to the standards of Britain of the time. The fact is that those standards would have been beneath the contempt of the Australian Aboriginal people, had they known the emotion of contempt, because the intruders came from a society that knew neither justice nor equality, neither freedom nor plenty while the Aboriginals enjoyed a freedom that has vanished from the earth, and a plenty rare in human history.

The average Aboriginal [Geoffrey Blainey says] *had in a typical year a variety of food such as even a rich Londoner couldn't hope to put on his table. The Aboriginal cultivated not one plant and tended not one animal. The Aboriginal lived well, but by moving around, not constantly but frequently and regularly. Even in the dry inland around Alice Springs, seventy or eighty different plant foods formed the diet of the Aboriginals. Further north, in Arnhem Land, the diet was richer and even more varied.*

Had their prejudices allowed them to recognise it, the first European settlers had the unique experience of seeing a lifestyle, that of the nomadic hunter-gatherer, preserved by isolation in Australia for thousands and thousands of years, and about to vanish forever. But as they helped it on its way to extinction, they gave no thought to the limbo its survivors would enter for generations.

AN ACCOUNTING ▲

▲ A BIG COUNTRY

OPPOSITE PAGE: *SUNSET IN THE ALLIGATOR RIVERS AREA, NT.*

Geoffrey Blainey holds that though the Aboriginal people neither farmed land nor husbanded animals, they had one great tool of food production they used with such skill and over such millennia that they changed the face of Australia. That tool was fire, and Blainey leans towards the belief that it was the 'farming fires' of the Aboriginals that may have created great grassland plains later to be of such value to European animal keepers. That view turns around the traditional belief that the Australian Aboriginal lived at the mercy of the land. It suggests, rather, that he dominated it by his understanding of nature. 'Fire,' says Blainey, 'was the core of Aboriginal technology.'

But of course it was quite foreign to the settlers from the old world, as was so much else about their new and unhappy home, and there could be no question of their learning anything from the 'primitive blacks'. So no-one recognised that the Aboriginal people stayed fit and healthy while the newcomers were dying of malnutrition when supplies from home failed to arrive. The food was under their noses, yet they starved. And when they set out to create a pretence of home with their imported trees and plants and furry animals, they wished upon those who would follow them such prizes as Paterson's Curse and the rabbit, prickly pear and foxes.

The time will come, Geoffrey Blainey believes, when Australians, white and black, will celebrate an Australia Day that records the true first settlement of the country, by people unknown at a time unrecorded. No point, he says, in searching the archives and the relics of Europe for our history. No good studying the temples and monuments that suggest European man is much older than man in Australia.

'Many achievements were taking place in Australia long before the pyra-

AN ACCOUNTING ▲

▲ *A BIG COUNTRY*

mids were built, long before the Parthenon was built. We won't really learn to understand Australian history until we get the right time clock.'

Thus Geoffrey Blainey puts a new side of our history. The bushman and poet Bill Harney, who lived among Aboriginal people most of his life, said something similar in elegant verse:

Not monuments to some king's vanished glory,
But flints and shards record man's greatest story.
Some husks and shells beside the grinding stones,
A painted cave, or etchings scratched on bones.
Debris on the floor of sheltering caves,
Or where erosion throws up ancient graves,
There find a story of that lowly one who first made fire,
He who made the sun to cast aside night's horror
Set man free,
To conquer unknown lands, to brave the sea.

OPPOSITE PAGE: OLD LAND, NEW ANIMALS: NOURLANGIE ROCK, NT.

It's Nice That You Don't Know the Future

Warren Gorge near Quorn, SA.

OPPOSITE PAGE: *'For a young country, a remarkable capacity to produce ruins.'*

For the young country that we so often tell ourselves we are, we have a remarkable capacity to produce ruins.

In the space of a couple of hundred years we've produced ruins in worse repair than some of the ruins of Europe and Asia that have stood for millennia. And we've had no great sackings to contend with, no Attila the Hun or Alexander the Great. The razing of sections of our cities is a recent phenomenon, carried out in the name of development by people who leave no traces. Unlike the great vandals of history, today's Attilas haul the evidence of their work away to the dump. Their contracts require a 'clean site'.

But in the bush, Nature is the demolisher, slower certainly than bulldozer and wrecking ball, wearing away at the edges of our old structures rather than bringing them crashing down, leaving not a clean site but sad standing traces that are often memorials to great hopes gone wrong or proof of failure to understand a new land.

Maybe they didn't build too well. Maybe the elements here attack with a ferocity unknown in other places, and a structure jerry-built through lack of money or lack of time, falls early victim. Maybe it was all intended to be temporary anyway, the builders distrusting the land they hardly knew, underestimating the severity, length and frequency of drought, failing to realise until it was too late that for much of Australia, drought is the norm, rain the exception. By their very presence, and the nature of the animals that they brought with them, they disturbed a fragile soil. Their European knowledge and experience was wrong for this place, but

AN ACCOUNTING ▲

▲ A BIG COUNTRY

by the time they found that out, it was already too late for huge areas of the country.

It was certainly too late for Kanyaka Station in South Australia's Flinders Ranges, a huge holding stretching from Willochra to Hawker in one of the most scenically beautiful parts of South Australia. Beautiful, but fragile. Perhaps it should just have been looked at, admired, rather than worked, but sheep were unleashed upon it and they ate and trampled it to death. Phillips, the owner of the original land grant, had seventy families living on and working Kanyaka when times were good, among them shepherds each with an area to graze and 2000 sheep to mind, and one contact with the outside world each month, when a man made the rounds from the homestead with rations.

Phillips used the local stone to build his homestead, and for seven shillings and six pence a week for skilled men, and rations only for labourers, he built a homestead he might well have thought would last forever. But it was abandoned, derelict and a ruin, in not much more than one lifetime.

What went wrong?

At Kanyaka and many other places like it, the Big Country was wrongly read. Daniel Keneally, bush poet and amateur historian:

The owners of the station came from England. They came out here, and they had some money, and they came up into the northern areas which was a great place at the time, blackfellers about, grass two and three feet [about half a metre to one metre] *high out on the plains and they thought this was the land of milk and honey.*

They didn't understand the climate, of course; the only men who did were the Aborigines. I suppose they laughed to themselves when they saw the settlers coming. They knew what was in the future.

There were quite a lot of blacks when my parents came here, but they soon got chased way back into the north-west and there they remained. Never came back again.

The New Chum owners of the huge sheep station had problems enough, but the real problems of this land began when politics, government, stepped in. By one of those acts of crass stupidity that occur when politics ventures into areas it knows nothing about, a political decision was made that Kanyaka should be subdivided. It would be split up into one-square-mile blocks, 259 hectares, which make such a neat pattern on the map on a bureaucrat's wall in a far away city, but make no concessions whatever to practicalities, realities, topography and climate.

That decision would destroy this land. And more: it would condemn men and women to wasted lives of hard work, poverty and despair as they tried to farm the unfarmable, because, by an administrative decision even more stupid than the subdivision, Authority demanded that part of each block be plowed and sown to wheat every year. Bush was cleared, crops planted. There were a couple of good seasons and congratulations were exchanged on this bold and successful experiment. More land was cleared, bigger areas planted, and then the climate returned to the normal, drought. The winds came and the land blew away, there was nothing to hold it.

'Some of the loveliest sandstorms you ever saw in your life,' Dan Keneally said mockingly of the hot north winds that stripped the living topsoil and carried it far enough away to top dress the Southern Ocean.

'The storms came up the plain, up from Quorn, across Willochra. And they had all colours as they came and rolled over and over. It's calm just as they come and then the wind hits you, whistling and howling, and it cuts low, can cut a paddock of feed off in one night.

'"Only a madman would live here," one old chap told me. But he lived here. He was born here.'

The story of Kanyaka Station is a story of the ruthlessness of nature towards those who defy it. It is a story of institutional stupidity, of individual and collective ignorance. It is also a story of our stewardship of a Big Country, and it is timely amid the self-congratulations of the Bi-Centennial to ask at what cost two centuries of European colonisation of Australia have been achieved.

The answer is enough to spoil the gaiety of the national birthday party. It is an accounting from which those who were the pioneers emerge flawed, but with the excuse of ignorance. We have no such excuse. We know the extent of the problems and we even know the answers. We therefore emerge condemned: we have changed the face of nearly three-quarters of Australia in that the natural growth has been in some way changed since 1788, natural species of both plants and animals reduced, endangered, or wiped out altogether.

Two-thirds of Australia's natural forests have been cut down and their destruction is gaining momentum rather than being slowed. Three-quarters of our rainforests are gone. Gross overclearing has upset the ecological balance of huge areas. No trees, therefore no birds. No birds, therefore more insect pests. More insects, less pasture. Less pasture, more pressure on what remains. More pressure, more stress.

The warning voices are heard, but ignored, for their warnings fly in the face of continuing profit, and the dedicated defence of profit is an Australian ethos. The Australian Conservation Foundation says bluntly now that our agri-

OPPOSITE PAGE: *ARTEFACTS OF THE AGE OF POWER AND WEALTH IN A PLACE OF PRE-HISTORY, RECORDING A COLONISATION THAT WAS MORE INVASION THAN SETTLEMENT.*
JIM FRAZIER/MANTIS WILDLIFE

AN ACCOUNTING ▲

▲ A BIG COUNTRY

cultural system is simply not sustainable in the long term. The garden will become barren unless we change our treatment of it, and soon. But while we continue to drag the last tonne of wheat out of marginal country that shouldn't be trying to grow wheat, while we tear the last woodchip out of a natural forest that will take generations to recover, while we, or others with our permission, sweep clean the sea of marketable fish species, then there is something hollow in our celebration of the last two centuries.

Let us take a statistical ten hectares of our Big Country, our Homeland. About six of those hectares have been damaged by erosion; wind and/or water have stripped the productive topsoil layer away, or substantially reduced its productive capacity. That's because we have used British and European farming methods and farm animals here, and this place was not designed for them. And don't forget the rabbit, and the huge erosion he's caused. Again, Australia was not designed for the rabbit. We brought him here.

Of our eroded six hectares, three need soil structural work to repair the damage. Nature, and our care, might fix the rest. Repairs will be expensive, far more than most of the land is worth. And as we, the imaginary owners of ten hectares, can't afford to spend that much money to put right the damage done, can Australia afford to spend an incalculable amount to put the whole country back the way it was?

But that's the wrong question. The right question is, can we afford not to? Going on the way we are, there will be not a lot to celebrate at the Tri-Centennial in 2088. Every hectare of Australia used for cropping is losing topsoil at rates varying from fifty to more than 250 tonnes a year. Well short of the Tri-Centennial, in less than fifty years in fact, there will be no topsoil left on more than 400 000 hectares of our wheat belt. That land will be dead, it will never grow anything again, and today's arguments over market share and export competition will sound hollow indeed.

In our most fertile lands, the irrigation areas, an aggrieved Nature is striking back: soil salinity, the product of thoughtless clearing and constant irrigation, is said to affect more than four million hectares, and in the vast Murray Darling Basin, it is already an ecological disaster.

One final note on the national birthday card: bushfire means to us destruction and the risk of death. But bushfire to Australia is part of the natural system. The Aboriginal people knew that and let the land burn when it was ready. With wet bag and hose and Bush Fire Brigade, we've done our best to stop fires, and we've done pretty well. Trouble is, we've got in the way of Nature and, without the control of fire, plants we don't want grow unimpeded, shrubs and grasses of no use to human or beast now cover more than 2 400 000 hectares. The job of eradication is so enormous it is unlikely ever to be attempted. We've lost, again.

'It's nice that you don't know the future,' said Dan Keneally, the bush poet. It was just as well, he meant, that the settlers of the Flinders Ranges didn't know their plans would fail, their future was without hope, their presence so short, their traces marked only by the ruins of their buildings.

It's hard to be poetic about people who do have pointers to the future by reading the signs of the present, yet who ignore the signs, disregard the knowledge, gag the warnings in the interests of short-term gain. Such people are unlikely to be fondly remembered at the time of the Tri-Centennial. The future will, more than likely, give them the same disregard that they, now, are giving the future.

The Track Behind, the Track Ahead

The vast machine and the miner's hard hat worn by the little boy were once symbols of an easy Australian future. Can we be so sure any more?
AUSTRALIAN PICTURE LIBRARY

OPPOSITE PAGE: *Boxes of bright cloth and coloured beads and axes: borrowing to keep the imports coming.*
AUSTRALIAN PICTURE LIBRARY

It is unlikely that a television program looking for a title now would call itself *A Big Country*. That was a title for more confident times; it described ourselves to ourselves, in terms which in the late 'sixties were, even if boastful, supportably and demonstrably true.

We had just found that the thin though highly productive and profitable skin of farmland we lived on was stretched over a hugely rich layer of mineral fat. The last of the old-style prospectors, Lang Hancock, had discovered in Western Australia that half the State seemed made of iron ore. Others had discovered that what gaps there were in the iron ore lodes were filled with nickel. And that was only the west. In the east, a layer of agricultural overburden concealed the world's greatest accessible deposits of high-grade coal, enough to keep the furnaces of the world alight for centuries. There would be gold and diamonds and wealth forever. The future was clearly boundless, or so we were told. The one-time providores to the world would change bushman's hat for hard hat and that would be all we needed to be the future quarrymasters to the world.

They lied to us. Or to be kinder to them, they told us what they thought, and their thoughts were based on nothing more secure than hope. On a foundation of hope was built expectation. From expectation came promises, from promises came certainty. From certainty came neglect of things productive. The manufacturers, the makers, the creators of substance went into decline, to be replaced in the pecking order of national business by traders in

AN ACCOUNTING ▲

paper, people and corporations who produced nothing. We had, in the meantime, stayed with outmoded institutions, maintained quaint and quite useless traditions, swallowed a line about duty and responsibility (always to others, never to ourselves), and were volunteered enthusiastically by our leaders for other people's wars. And we had grovelled more than a bit in the belief that that was the way to sustain friendships.

Then, suddenly, we were on our own. Mother England had taken a number of European lovers who were keeping her fed. Uncle Sam had set up shop in competition with ours and was cutting prices. The European politicians were frantically buying voters by way of agricultural subsidies. And we found ourselves locked into too few markets with too few products. Our new friends, once we'd kissed and made up after that unpleasantness of the 1940s, were only too happy to go on selling us bright cloth, coloured beads and axes, but they really didn't want to dig our quarries so deep any more, because they had found other people had quarries that were as good or better, and cheaper to boot. Our problem was that we had acquired a simple people's addiction to cloth and beads and axes and wanted to go on getting them. So the tribal elders borrowed on our behalf and the beads and axes keep on coming until one day...

Now we have learned that assets are worth only what someone else is prepared to pay for them: no buyer, no value. And the supply of buyers for what we have to sell has been constricting for years but we had nothing new to offer.

We had listened to false prophets for some decades too long, believed and relied upon alien experts and corrupted expertise only too willing to assure us, for reasons of their own, that we couldn't process wool, build cars, make aeroplanes, produce computers. We had a list of lost opportunities a century long. We were in deep trouble. We would no longer call a television program, boastfully, *A Big Country*.

Yet, more than ever now, we need to know ourselves, and no matter what it's called, a television program in the style of *A Big Country* remains necessary. The program, and the people who made it, were the only proven documentary production unit the ABC had and, even should the name change, and the theme music, and the titles be replaced in television's endless search for the new for the sake of the new, a program by Australians about Australians will continue. And it will be made, if not by the same people, then by the same kind of people.

It is entirely possible that young men and women who were not born when *A Big Country* began, and who have just about finished school now, will photograph, direct, edit, write and sound-record future versions of this venerable program. It might be called something different, but the essence will be there, and such programs will continue while ever one person has an interest in knowing something about the life of another.

For twenty years, *A Big Country* demonstrated that interest exists. Its people changed, its thrust changed with them, for the changing fashions of television reflect more the game of musical chairs in television management than the changing taste of the television consumer, the people who watch.

For seventeen of its twenty years, *A Big Country* had the same manager, a record unique in the television industry in Australia. John Sparkes, a rural broadcaster most of his working life, was the foundation executive producer of *A Big Country*. Inevitably, the program reflected his tastes. The big turnover in program-makers reflected the lack of unanimous agreement with those tastes.

When no longer in direct command, but exercising an administrative control, John Sparkes held to his old principle: find good stories, and tell them well. Do that, and people will watch, year in, year out, as they did for two decades. The television viewer doesn't demand things. He/she accepts or rejects what is offered by television managements and the measure of success or failure is the system of audience evaluation called 'the ratings'.

A new piece of technical wizardry will soon be added to some television sets. It's called the People Meter, and it promises to tell, for the first time, who's watching what and when. The ratings may be turned end for end, and along with them the whole television industry, because never before has it been possible to measure an audience except through the highly fallible factor of memory and the questionably honest factor of answers to questions on a printed form. The People Meter will apply the equivalent of continuous polling to television watchers, and it will give the industry the good or the bad news. It is highly likely then that the future of such television programs as *A Big Country* will be decided by a black box plugged into television sets all over the land, and that is as it should be, provided the sampling is fair.

The future of the Big Country itself is more difficult to measure. No black box can tell us that, and, fortunately, though the trends are here to see, the next twenty years lie beyond the scope of this book and this writer. But we will have to live them, and let us remember as we do that the span of our history as seen and reported by this unique television program in tracing our present and our past has also pointed the way of the future.

Though it makes no pretence of being a guide to where we're going, it has given us over twenty years a perspective of where we've been and how we've got here. That's been the value of *A Big Country*.